TERRA NOVA

BY TED TALLY

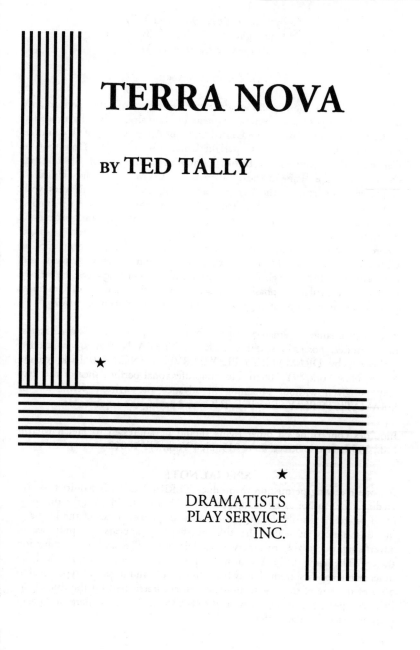

DRAMATISTS
PLAY SERVICE
INC.

TERRA NOVA was first presented at the Yale School of Drama, in New Haven, Connecticut, on March 10, 1977. The cast was as follows:

SCOTT .... Douglas Simes
AMUNDSEN .... Barry Press
KATHLEEN .... Marianne Owen
BOWERS .... Tony Sherer
OATES .... Rob Dean
WILSON .... Timothy Hagan
EVANS .... David Marshall Grant

After subsequent revision, the play was performed at the 1977 National Playwrights Conference, at the O'Neill Theatre Center.

The professional premiere was at the Yale Repertory Theatre, on November 18, 1977. The cast was as follows:

SCOTT .... Arthur Hill
AMUNDSEN .... Michael Higgins
KATHLEEN .... Lindsay Crouse
BOWERS .... Jeremy Geidt
OATES .... Michael Gross
WILSON .... Max Wright
EVANS .... Stephen Rowe

Both Yale productions were directed by Travis Preston, with scenery and costumes designed by Jess Goldstein, lighting by Robert Jared, and projections by William Warfel.

CHARACTERS

SCOTT. "They'll remember me, all right, for about five years, my name on some bloody little plaque in the fifth-floor lavatory at the Admiralty."

AMUNDSEN. "Think of the details."

KATHLEEN. "You know the place, right along where the river flows into the sea."

BOWERS. "Scoff all you want, my lad, but this theory of mine explains many puzzling and wondrous things."

WILSON. "Gentlemen, I've one last cigar that I'd been saving for this moment . . . And I say, to hell with the Norskers, I'm going to smoke it anyway."

OATES. "I'm a soldier, aren't I? And all a soldier needs to know is his duty."

EVANS. "I thought it'd be worth a hand for that—to go to the Pole. To be one of the first."

In the winter of 1911–1912, five Englishmen and five Norwegians raced each other to the bottom of the earth. Only the five Norwegians returned.

This is the story of the Englishmen.

For Bob and Florence

PRODUCTION NOTES

No attempt should be made at the literal representation of an Antarctic landscape, yet this should be *suggested*, both in its starkness and its beauty. The setting above all should be simple and flexible, close to a bare stage.

A possible example: across the extreme upstage edge of the playing area a ship's spar is suspended high in the air. Attached to this beam by means of hemp rigging is a vast piece of rough white fabric which spills down in tortuous drapes to the stage, then unrolls across the playing space itself and over the edge on to the auditorium floor. On the stage this cloth is bunched and stiffened into ridges. Where it soars into the air, this cloth will be useful for various effects of lighting, such as the *Aurora Australis* in Act II, as well as for the slide projections, which will appear distorted on the uneven surface. It is translucent, and will allow for back-lighting and sihouette effects. The look of this huge cloth suggests snow, sails, or shrouds, all at once. Around it the stage is darkened to create a black box effect; entrances and exits are concealed in the shadows, and orientation is difficult.

In contrast to the abstraction of such a setting, hand properties such as the sextant, and small set pieces such as the stove, should be as grittily realistic as possible. The tent called for in the camp scenes may be nothing more than a simple cutout of canvas, open towards the audience and roofless, like an angled wall. The bamboo supports of this canvas can be set into holes drilled through the ground cloth. All properties not carried by the men themselves must come from, and be returned to, the sled. The sled is approximately six feet long, two feet wide, and six inches high above waxed metal or wooden runners. Numerous supply boxes, mostly wooden and wrapped in canvas, are lashed on to the sled. It is pulled by means of long leather traces buckled to its front. The tent, when not in use, is rolled up and strapped on top of the sled.

Scott and his men, except when otherwise noted, wear a loose approximation of real Antarctic gear, circa 1911. This would include: thick sweaters under baggy parkas, knitted caps or balaclavas, and pants that look like heavy wool tucked into furry boots. When not in the tent they all wear bulky mittens, attached by long strips of canvas to harnesses around their chests. When removed the mittens dangle from these harnesses. When the men are hauling the sled, they can free their hands by clipping the sled traces to the backs of their harnesses. On the march, they may also wear sun goggles. Their skin, where exposed, is quite sun-bronzed. They've made a conscious effort to keep their hair and whiskers neatly trimmed, though this appearance, like their general physical condition, will deteriorate rapidly in Act II.

SLIDES

Photographic slides such as those referred to in the text are under copyright and may only be used with special permission and, in most circumstances, considerable expense. In professional productions of the play they have been painstakingly tracked down, assembled, and rented at such photographic services as the Bettman Archives in New York City. The author feels, however, that the play can stand without them, and amateurs may be best advised to avoid their use.

SONGS

For the guidance of groups producing *Terra Nova* the songs included in the text of the play are as follows:

In Act I the first song which the men sing is a traditional chantey entitled "Drunken Sailors." Later on, in the same act, they sing "Men of Harlech," a song which is sometimes referred to as the Welsh National Anthem.

In Act II *Evans* sings "Eternal Father, Strong to Save," a traditional Protestant hymn which is also known as the "Sailor's Hymn."

The Play service cannot supply copies of these songs, but they should be available through music stores in most cities.

So far as I can venture to offer an opinion on such a matter, the purpose of our being in existence, the highest object that human beings can set before themselves, is not the pursuit of any such chimera as the annihilation of the unknown; but it is simply the unwearied endeavour to remove its boundaries a little further from our sphere of action.

Thomas Huxley

(From Scott's Antarctic journal)

PROLOGUE

Darkness and silence.

Time passes. A shudder of wind. Pause. Again.

Suddenly, an image appears, huge against a cyclorama, filling the entire back of the stage. It towers over our heads. The image is a black-and-white photograph, rear-projected. It show a vast moonlit seascape, the water filled with chunks of ice. Now a series of such photographs will flash in succession. Each will brighten for a moment, then fade:

A three-masted steamship at sea. We see it in full-length silhouette, an ominous dark shape without detail. It is Scott's ship, the Terra Nova.

The same ship, now in heavy seas. We look forward from amidships. Sailors in sou'westers are manning pumps on the port side.

(Again the strange windsong is heard, chill and stronger, rising sharply in pitch before subsiding again.)

The ship trapped in pack ice. It looms huge in the foreground. Two men stand on the ice near the bow.

The ship is now quite far away. The foreground is filled with ice and water. (The wind is a cry of rage or pain, coming closer and growing louder.)

The ship is so far away we can no longer see it. We see only an endless plain of ice.

Then a long, grey mountain range, with snow-capped peaks.

Then a tortured surface where drifts of snow have been whipped into frozen waves.

Then a vast panorama in which the only perceivable detail can be found in the sky, which is grey-streaked and threatening. There is no part of these final images which offers any human comfort or shelter whatsoever.

The last slide holds, as simultaneously the wind is full upon us. It shrieks to impossible towers of sound. It is awesome, deafening — the fabric of the air itself torn apart in the hands of giants.

As the sound smashes against us, the final slide brightens and brightens until finally it shows no contrasts at all, but is just a blank square of light, as if the photograph itself had been burned away by a pure white flame.

As the slide whitens and the wind howls, a spot slowly creates a pool of light C., *and in this pool is revealed the figure of a man — who is Scott himself. He wears Antarctic clothing. He is kneeling on one knee, hunched over rigidly. Using a pencil, he is writing in a small notebook balanced on his knee. The effort of writing is enormously difficult for him; he seems battered by the wind. Now as the wind reaches its peak, he looks slowly up and stares out at us. His features are strained and weary. The wind continues to whipsaw impossibly louder and louder until suddenly it stops, as abruptly and cleanly as if sliced with an axe. There is a silence which seems more deafening than the wind, and Scott still kneels as before.*

SCOTT. (*Softly.*) Message to the Public. The causes of the disaster are these. (*He does not move, and the light on him does not fade.*)

TERRA NOVA

ACT I

As Scott returns to his writing, a spot comes up on Amundsen,
very dapper in white tie and tails

AMUNDSEN. Ladies and gentlemen! Distinguished guests.
And my fellow members of the Royal Geographical Society. I
believe that concludes out lantern programme at this time. I feel
certain that our speaker for tonight needs little introduction
from me. (*He looks at Scott, smiles.*) Therefore! Let me hasten to
present—England's own hero of the Antarctic—Captain
Robert—Falcon—Scott! (*Amundsen gestures broadly, as additional
spots hit Scott. An expectant silence.*)

SCOTT. (*Writing, with difficulty.*) I do not think human beings
ever came through such a month as we have come
through . . . And we should have succeeded—in spite of the
weather—except—except for the . . . I can't make—my hands.
(*To Amundsen, helplessly.*) I can't move the pencil.(*Amundsen is
embarrassed. Slight pause. He gestures again, more grandly.*)

AMUNDSEN. Captain—Scott!

SCOTT. How am I to write if I can't move the pencil?

AMUNDSEN. (*In a stage whisper.*) Scott—what's the matter?

SCOTT. What?

AMUNDSEN. Are you ill, man? Are you indisposed?

SCOTT. No, no, I just—my hands.

AMUNDSEN. Really, this is most irregular. (*He smiles reassur-
ingly to the audience.*) The members are waiting.

SCOTT. (*Peering out.*) They're . . .

AMUNDSEN. Waiting. We're all waiting. To hear.

SCOTT. Ah! (*Pause.*) To hear?

ADMUNDSEN. About the race.

SCOTT. Ah yes. Yes. (*Bitterly.*) Everyone loves a race.

AMUNDSEN. Mustn't disappoint them, Scott. So many wanting to know.

SCOTT. It's just my hands, don't you see. And only— if I might rest now for a bit, because I'm so frightfully tired.

AMUNDSEN. (*Evenly.*) Not now, old man. After.

SCOTT. After, yes. (*Pause.*) Afterwards I may rest? (*A spot comes up on Kathleen, U. from Scott. She is a pretty woman in her early thirties, wearing a light, flowing summer dress. Her hair is up, set for a party.*)

KATHLEEN. Con? Is something the matter?

SCOTT. (*Still kneeling, facing out.*) Kathleen! My hands—I can't feel the pencil. And yet this fellow says—says . . .

KATHLEEN. Why don't you come in now? It's getting dark.

SCOTT. No, no, Kath—listen to me, there isn't much time. I have to tell you—about the most extraordinary *place* I've been.

KATHLEEN. Oh yes.

SCOTT. The things I've seen there! Terrible and wonderful! Flames exploding in air.

KATHLEEN. Mountains of crystal . . .

SCOTT. Colors falling from the sky.

KATHLEEN. Yes.

SCOTT. Silence, like a scream into wind.

KATHLEEN. Silence like sleep.

SCOTT. Like sleep, yes.

KATHLEEN. Like a dream.

SCOTT. So many things to tell—but my hands . . .

KATHLEEN. Con? We're going to have a son.

SCOTT. A son . . .

KATHLEEN. Last night when I woke I knew. I crept out and ran down to the beach. I swam out quietly, in a calm sea, as far as my strengh would take me.

SCOTT. Kath, I can't write any longer . . .

KATHLEEN. I floated with my face turned up to the moon. I thought, "my son will love the nights, and he will love the sea".

SCOTT. Tell him—tell our boy that I said . . .

KATHLEEN. Yes.

SCOTT. That I said . . .(*His voice trails off.*)

AMUNDSEN. (*Delicately, after a pause.*) The Captain has, I believe, a most unusual and —ah, a most *important*—announcement to make to us at this time. And so now, without any futher ado, I give you—Robert Scott. (*There is a sound of wind, softly.*

Scott looks about, as if aware for the first time of his surroundings, his audience. He rises with slow determination, moves downstage and faces front. He removes his mittens and pulls off his balaclava. Amundsen exits. Kathleen watches Scott closely.)

SCOTT. My fellow members of the Society. (*Loudly and firmly.*) We are all engaged, all of us here in this room tonight, in a great scientific race, in which our national pride is at stake. No human footprints have yet appeared at the South Geographic Pole. When they do first appear — and I assure you that day is very close — I intend that they shall be British footprints! My new ship, the *Terra Nova*, will steam down the Thames on the morning of May thirtieth, and her destination is Antarctica. I *am* going back, I am going to try a second time — and this time I shall not return until I've planted the Union Jack on the bottom of the earth! (*Towards the end of the above, there is the sound of lusty singing approaching. Scott's men — Bowers, Wilson, Oates and Evans are singing a chantey.*)

<table>
<tr><td></td><td></td><td>What shall we do with a drunken sailor?</td></tr>
<tr><td></td><td></td><td>What shall we do with a drunken sailor?</td></tr>
<tr><td></td><td></td><td>What shall we do with a drunken sailor,</td></tr>
<tr><td>BOWERS</td><td></td><td>Ear-ly in the mor-nin'?</td></tr>
<tr><td>WILSON</td><td>*singing*</td><td>Put 'em in the scuppers with a hosepipe</td></tr>
<tr><td>OATES</td><td>*together*</td><td>on 'em,</td></tr>
<tr><td>EVANS</td><td>*offstage*</td><td>Put 'em in the scuppers with a hosepipe</td></tr>
<tr><td></td><td></td><td>on 'em,</td></tr>
<tr><td></td><td></td><td>Put 'em in the scuppers with a hosepipe</td></tr>
<tr><td></td><td></td><td>on 'em,</td></tr>
<tr><td></td><td></td><td>Ear-ly in the mor-nin'!</td></tr>
</table>

(*By the end of the second stanza of the chantey, Bowers, Wilson, Oates and Evans enter, hauling their sled. Bowers, Wilson and Oates are in the lead, hauling on leather traces. Evans trails, pushing. The sled is very heavy, and awkward to move. It is piled high with supply boxes and lashed over with tarpaulin. As the men enter, Kathleen turns and goes. The lights cover the entire stage. Bowers spots an obstruction in their path, as they reach* C.)

BOWERS. (*breathlessly.*) Whoa! Bit of a crack here! (*They stop. All but Evans come forward and kneel to examine the "crack" which bars their way. Evans sits on the back of the sled, grateful to catch his breath.*)

OATES. That's not a crack. That's another bleeding crevasse.

BOWERS. There's a thin crust over it.

WILSON. (*To Bowers.*) Can you see bottom, Birdie?

BOWERS. (*Lordly.*) I can see a Chinaman, on his way up.

(*As Scott speaks again, they kneel in silence, studying the ground. They are not certain that the ice immediately ahead of them will bear the weight of the sled.*)

SCOTT. (*Still facing front; continuing his speech.*) There is another man who will attempt the race. I mean the Norwegian, Roald Amundsen. Listen to the means by which our Mr. Amundsen thinks fit to achieve the Pole. He intends to take along huge teams of dogs, whip them into hauling his men overland to the Great Barrier Glacier, then slaughter them when he has no further use for them and feed on the fresh dog meat! Well. I leave it to you to decide how sporting that is. (*Oates sighs and gets up.*)

OATES. Help me pull us up to the edge. Come on, Birdie, put your scrawny little back to it. (*They pick up the traces again.*) Together—one! Two! Three! (*They heave at the lines, straining mightily, but the sled will not budge. They collapse, puffing.*)

SCOTT. My own men have trained until they're in the peak of condition, and we intend to march it on foot.

OATES. Nothing. Stuck again.

WILSON. The runners are iced up. (*They rest on the sled, catching their breath.*)

SCOTT. To the Pole and back—on foot!

WILSON. (*Wearily.*) There's only one thing for it.

BOWERS. Go back two hundred miles and turn starboard, 'stead of port.

OATES. Build a bridge of ice.

BOWERS. Wait here for the spring thaw—'cept there isn't any.

WILSON. Thank you. No, I mean we'll have to unload again. (*The others groan noisily.*)

OATES. Unload! You're off your chump. (*He chops at the ice around the base of the runners.*)

SCOTT. Only we English cound so believe in an ideal . . .

BOWERS. Nothing like the army, is it, Titus?

OATES. Cavalry, not army!

BOWERS. All the same to me, mate.

WILSON. (*Sarcastically.*) Let's just *talk* it across!

SCOTT. Only we will so achieve it . . .

OATES. Well, I say it's bloody stupid to unload if we can yank it!

BOWERS. And I say we just bloody well tried that, didn't we?

OATES. Then let's ask the Captain!

BOWERS. Fine!

WILSON. Yes, Robert—what do you say?

SCOTT. (*Still facing front.*) Not with cheap tricks, or cruelty to brute beasts, but with the pride of English manhood!

WILSON. (*After a slight pause.*) Robert, did you hear me? (*Scott turns and stares at them.*)

SCOTT. What?

OATES. The crevasse.

BOWERS. Do we yank or unload, Captain?

SCOTT. (*After a pause.*) Yes, yes, of course. (*He goes to them briskly.*) Wilson, Bowers, slip your traces back along the sides. Foot the back ends of the runners and when I signal, pull like the devil. The rest of us lifting the front corners. Ready? Heave! (*They all tug together; the front end of the sled is slowly lifted a few inches and yanked forward, after a tremendous effort. They once again catch their breath, Bowers half-collapsing over the side of the sled.*) You see how simple it is, Bowers? We've moved it all of eight inches further along, and all it's cost you is the chance ever to have children.

BOWERS. (*Grimacing.*) If you're referring to that ungodly popping noise, that was Mr. Oates, thank you. My last one blew a hundred miles back.

OATES. The footing is better on this side.

WILSON. I hope to God we've seen the last of that soft powder.

BOWERS. Well—let's get on with it, then. (*Passing Scott.*) Ev'nin', Captain. Lovely weather for ducks! (*They drag the sled rather easily now, over the stage and off. Evans, pushing, must struggle a bit to keep up.*)

EVANS. (*Puffing, as he passes Scott.*) Ev'nin', sir.

SCOTT. Evans.

(*Bowers, Wilson and Evans exit, singing. Oates lingers at the edge of the stage. In the distance we hear the sound of singing again, gradually trailing off.*)

BOWERS
WILSON } (*offstage*)
EVANS

Hoo-ray and up he rises!
Hoo-ray and up he rises!
Hoo-ray and up he rises,
Ear-ly in the mor-nin'!

(*Scott looks at Oates curiously.*)

OATES. Captain Scott—may I have a word with you?

SCOTT. Certainly, Oates.

OATES. It's Evans, sir.

SCOTT. What about him?

OATES. (*Reluctantly.*) Well, he's not pulling his weight, sir.

SCOTT. (*Surprised.*) Evans?

OATES. Yes, sir. He tires easily for a big man. I don't like it.

SCOTT. Do you mean he's shirking?

OATES. No, but he's slowing the pace, that's certain, and he favors his left hand.

SCOTT. I see. Put him on point so he can rest a bit, but don't let him see he's getting any sort of special attention. If you can, get a look at that hand. I don't like the sound of that. (*Pause.*) I won't have the pace slowed, Oates. We've got to do five more miles this afternoon.

OATES. (*Grinning.*) We'll do five easily enough, Captain. We'll do eight. We're all in good spirits.

SCOTT. I can depend on you, Oates.

OATES. It's not me. All I have to do is mention the Norwegians, and they fairly fly.

SCOTT. Splendid. Well then, that's all, Oates. Carry on.

OATES. Yes, sir. I mean aye aye, sir. (*He starts to go, then hesitates.*) Firmer crust here, Captain. Maybe things will start to look up, this side of the Beardmore.

SCOTT. I hope so, Oates. I sincerely do.

OATES. Yes sir. (*Pause.*) Well. (*Oates exits. The wind is heard softly. The lights fade to a spot on Scott. After a moment of uncertainty he faces out front again. During the following, Amundsen enters upstage, unseen.*)

SCOTT. In—conclusion—ladies and gentlemen. No journey ever made with dogs can approach that glory which is realized when a party of men go forth to face hardships unaided, and by days and weeks of splendid physical exertion, succeed in solving some problem of the great unknown. Our final victory over Norway will be all the sweeter, all the nobler, because we will know we've taken the prize by playing the game as it *ought* to be played! (*Scott concludes as if expecting a great ovation. Instead we hear only one pair of hands clapping, mockingly. Scott turns, is startled to see Amundsen revealed upstage behind the scrim. He now wears high boots and a huge dark coat with a bristling fur collar. The spot fades on Scott.*)

18

Light glows through the cyclorama; an eerie wash of color fills the stage. Amundsen stops clapping, and , after a pause, speaks. All trace of the M.C.'s manner is now gone: he speaks in his own harsh, slightly accented voice.)

AMUNDSEN. Success is a bitch. Grab her, and have her — but don't stand under her window with a mandolin. (*Scott turns, his eyes wander over the audience.*)

SCOTT. The explanations I have to go through, the flag-waving, even at the Society! They call themselves scientists, but for three years now their stinginess has frustrated my efforts to open a whole new *continent* for science.

AMUNDSEN. For science? What can that possibly have to do with you? (*He moves down through a slash in the scrim.*) A strange science, to tell you a thousand pound sled can be manhauled across sixteen hundred miles. (*Pause.*) I consult a chart and a caloric table. It tells me that on the eightieth day of my journey, according to precise schedule, the seventeenth animal must be converted to protein. And that is science.

SCOTT. Of a certain kind, perhaps.

AMUNDSEN. (*Shrugging.*) Two methods, one goal.(*Pause.*) Most men squander their chances. Their lives pass as if they slept — at the end a vague sadness, then . . . (*He makes a little gesture.*) But you — and me. How many in the world like us, eh? We concentrate, we wait — for what? One place, one turning. The pattern revealed. (*Pause.*) Suppose we could stand on another planet, English, and see our whole lives at once?

SCOTT. How like another planet it must feel to stand at the bottom of the earth.

AMUNDSEN. And what a moment to be there first. Oh yes. How many lifetimes would we give for that? (*Pause.*) You and me, we're the same, eh? But you act the fine gentleman, and I'm only a filthy barbarian. A killer of dogs.

SCOTT. I said nothing of the kind.

AMUNDSEN. A foreigner, then. It's the same thing to you.

SCOTT. You don't play the game.

AMUNDSEN. Oh yes, the English game. By which you mean that peculiar love affair between your race and Man's Best Friend. Shall I tell you a little secret? It's only the big ones I shoot. With the puppies I like to snap off the heads and drink the blood.

SCOTT. I don't find you very amusing. And you know precisely what I mean.

AMUNDSEN. Do I? Oh, yes. (*Pause.*) You're angry because I swore to take the North Pole, and leave the South to you.

SCOTT. Yes, damn it. You betrayed my trust for the shabby little advantage of a few weeks head start. You lied to me in front of the whole world!

AMUNDSEN. It wasn't a lie. I meant what I said, for as long as it was convenient. (*Pause.*) Oh, but I did want the North! More than you've ever wanted anything in your life. From the time I sat in the firelight and listened to tales of huge icecaps, where perhaps the gods still walked the earth . . . But you see — the American beat me there. Do you know what it is to see a dream strangled in newspaper cuttings? No . . . well, I can't see the point of being the second man in history to reach the North Pole — can you? (*Pause.*) I'm going South, English.

SCOTT. You're at liberty to try. A decent sense of courtesy towards a brother explorer is more than I have any right to expect.

AMUNDSEN. Think of it as a sporting gesture, Scott! Just a bit of healthy open-air competition. Isn't that part of playing your damned game? As for the dogs, I won't apologize for common sense. A husky is fifty pounds of dinner hauling you along until you need to eat it.

SCOTT. There *are* rules. Codes, standards, among civilized men! One doesn't cease behaving properly simply because one is entering a wilderness. All the more reason to set an example. (*Pause.*) You'll never understand. You're not English.

AMUNDSEN. But I do understand. Playing the game means treating your dogs like gentlemen, and your gentlemen like dogs. You're an infant, tickling yourself with a razor!

KATHLEEN. (*Off.*) Con?

AMUNDSEN. (*Urgently.*) Listen to me, English. Success is a bitch. You can grab her and have her if your plan is right — and that's all. Not because you made her swoon with your virtue. So learn a passion for details. That's not so romantic, but it can keep bread in your belly and your backside out of the snow. (*He turns to go.*)

SCOTT. Amundsen — wait! (*Kathleen appears, upstage. She carries a small wrapped gift in one hand.*)

AMUNDSEN. I *will* wait — in the one place I can afford to wait for a man as determined as you. In the meantime — think of the details.

SCOTT. Amundsen! (*He starts to go to Amundsen. Amundsen exits. Scott stands looking after him.*)

KATHLEEN. Con. You said you were going upstairs to rest.

SCOTT. I — couldn't sleep. (*Pause.*) I dreamt of Amundsen again.

KATHLEEN. Was he very frightening?

SCOTT. Frightening enough. I came down here. I wanted — I don't know what I wanted. (*The lights begin to soften, especially* U., *where it becomes quite dark. The wind fades, and is replaced by the sound of trickling water, as from a small fountain. Patterns of leafy shadow appear across the moonlit ground.*)

KATHLEEN. Why don't you come in now? (*Pause.*) They've all gone.

SCOTT. A moment more, that's all.

KATHLEEN. You'll get a chill.

SCOTT. No. No, I won't.

KATHLEEN. I brought this. (*He turns and sees the gift.*) I thought, as he won't take notice inside, I shall simply have to tackle him in the garden. (*She tosses it to him.*)

SCOTT. What is it?

KATHLEEN. Haven't the foggiest. (*Scott opens the package and removes a knitted scarf.*)

SCOTT. Kath, it's lovely.

KATHLEEN. And you thought I'd never prove domestic. Well, you see? I've made a birthday party, and I've knitted a scarf.

SCOTT. Will you put it round me?

KATHLEEN. I'll do better. I'll tie you up in it. (*She wraps the scarf round his shoulders, draws him close, kisses him fiercely. He breaks the embrace; a moment of silence.*)

SCOTT. Peter asleep?

KATHLEEN. Tucked in ages ago. Not before insisting on three stories. He was very cross because you didn't kiss him good night. You'll get a severe dressing-down in the a.m., I should think.

SCOTT. I'll look in on him later. You're not angry with me?

KATHLEEN. No. I made your apologies for you. Everyone quite understood how preoccupied you must be.

SCOTT. Did they. (*Pause.*) I've spoiled it for you. I've embarrassed you in front of your friends, haven't I?

KATHLEEN. Con, it was for you. I wanted you to enjoy your birthday. I wanted a big occasion.

SCOTT. Yes, well I like your artistic friends—really, very much—only I just don't have much patience for that society chatter. (*They laugh.*) 'Fraid I'll never make a go of it as a celebrity.

KATHLEEN. Oh nonsense, people are charmed by you. They all think it's terribly proper for an "explorer chappie" to be enigmatic and withdrawn.

SCOTT. Rude.

KATHLEEN. Withdrawn. (*Pause.*) It's lovely out. The air is so still. (*She sits, takes a breath.*) What's that smell, do you notice?

SCOTT. Lilacs. The whole place reeks of them, I can barely breathe.

KATHLEEN. Don't be so sentimental.

SCOTT. (*Sitting beside her.*) Look at it all, Kath. The goldfish pool, your sculptures, these bizarre flowers. It's the gaudiest terrace in Belgravia.

KATHLEEN. It is not gaudy. It's Italianate. (*He smiles, takes out a pipe and lights it.*) Are the stars as nice in the southern hemisphere? I suppose they're not the same ones at all. (*Pause.*) Is it really so different, looking at them with the world turned wrongside-up?

SCOTT. The air is so much cleaner. Makes them look larger, brighter somehow. Sometimes they actually sparkle, with those little points on them, like a drawing in one of Peter's books. Still. (*Pause.*) I've been happier here, I think, in this garden—than anywhere else in my life. Every flower in its place, I suppose.

KATHLEEN. But you will go back, and very soon. Won't you?

SCOTT. (*After a pause.*) Am I as obvious as that?

KATHLEEN. Obvious! When you can't eat, can't sleep—when you curse yourself a hundred times a day for some half-imagined clumsiness and won't look your own son in the eye, obvious, yes, I should say so! You've never had a thought that could keep itself from your face, Con.

SCOTT. Tell me you want me to throw it over and I shall. I promise you have only to say it, even now.

KATHLEEN. Yes, that would certainly make it easier. That would give you what you've been searching for. A reason not to go.

SCOTT. (*After a pause.*) We've only been married two years . . .

KATHLEEN. Yes.

SCOTT. And there's Peter—they can't expect . . .

KATHLEEN. No, of course not.

SCOTT. Well surely the press can see that, and the blessed British public. What in God's name do they want from me? I've been there already!

KATHLEEN. Half-way, yes. (*Pause.*) It isn't the press, Con. There are a thousand excuses sufficient for them. But not one sufficient for you.

SCOTT. You. (*Pause.*) You are sufficient for me.

KATHLEEN. (*Gently.*) No. You'd always measure me against what might have been. I'd always come out wanting. (*Pause.*) Well you're going back, of course you are. You're the best man for the job, anyone can see that. "Scott of the Antarctic!" But I wonder—is there a single person in this country who can guess how you actually despise that place?

SCOTT. Kath, I don't . . .

KATHLEEN. (*Angrily.*) Despise it, yes, and yourself, until you have it! Well, go back and take it! Go, or stay, Con, I don't care, I don't care, so long as you'll only be happy again. It's that I can't bear. You walk through your days like a man in a dream. I talk to you but you hear nothing. I look in your eyes and see nothing. I wonder who you are. (*Pause.*) And I am very much afraid I shall stop caring.

SCOTT. (*After a pause.*) Inside tonight at the party—it was full of ghosts, Kath. They all looked like me, but their faces were younger. (*He knocks the ash from his pipe and puts it away.*) When you lit the candles on the cake, I cringed with every flame. Forty-one charges. Forty-one counts of guilt by mediocrity. (*Pause.*) I ought to be in the Admiralty, Kath, a man my age, twenty-eight years of service—or at the very least a commodore on active duty. Duncan was a commodore at thirty-two! I'm not so certain any more they'd be willing to give me a flagship even if war came. Sometimes I think, what's the bloody use, I'll retire my commission, a captain's pension is not so bad. They think there's only one thing I'm good for, a damned half-pay land sailor, and getting a bit ragged even at that. (*In a bitter rush.*) Do you know what Bridgeman said to me the other day? He told me if I were applying for the first expedition nowadays, I'd be rejected for reason of age. Me! He meant it as a joke. "Younger men, plenty in line, awfully rigorous don't you know." I was *seething* — I told him the damned scheme would never have *existed* if it hadn't been for me, and he said yes, of course you *formed* it, old man — why your very name is sy*non*ymous with polar exploration, and they'll always remember you for that, and because after all you did get *so* close, what *was* it, only a few hundred miles out, topping good show *that* was, old sport, and I said yes, old sport, they'll remember me all right, for about two years, my name on some bloody little plaque in the fifth-floor lavatory at the Admiralty! (*He rushes to a halt, out of breath, lost in himself. After a long moment he looks up at her and takes her in.*) You're shivering.

KATHLEEN. It's terribly cold.

SCOTT. Take the scarf.

KATHLEEN. No, you keep it.

SCOTT. I don't need it. Here.

KATHLEEN. I said keep it.

SCOTT. (*Angrily.*) Will you just take the damned thing? (*She looks at him, miserable.*) Oh Christ, Kath. Oh Christ I'm sorry . . . (*Bowers enters upstage from Scott, sees him, and stops. Bowers and Kathleen do not see one another.*)

BOWERS. We're breaking the march and making camp. Are there any orders, sir? (*Scott turns and looks dully at Bowers.*)

KATHLEEN. I'm going back inside now, Con.

BOWERS. Are you coming, sir?

KATHLEEN. Come inside. Come to bed.

SCOTT. (*Confused.*) In — a bit. (*Bowers, concerned, takes a step or two towards Scott.*)

BOWERS. Are you all right, Captain?

KATHLEEN. Will you be all right out here?

SCOTT. Yes — if I could just — have some time.

BOWERS. Right, then, (*He moves away,* U. *He stops, looking off.*)

KATHLEEN. Good night. (*She turns to go.*)

24

SCOTT. Kath!

KATHLEEN. (*Stopping.*) Perhaps we shouldn't talk any more.

SCOTT. It isn't here for me, my love. I wish to God it were. I can't explain it or defend it. I can only beg you to think kindly of me. (*The sound of crickets fades and is replaced by a soft wind. Oates, Wilson, and Evans enter, hauling the sled. Bowers goes to help them. They begin to set up their camp for the night,* C., *unloading supplies from the sled. Their movements are brisk, practiced, and fluid, with no wasted effort. They put up a tent, with its* D. *side open to the audience. Wilson and Evans go inside the tent silently, and at once begin preparing a stew for dinner, using a large pot on a small portable stove. They sit on wooden crates, huddled close to the stove for warmth. Oates and Bowers remain outside the tent. They remove supply crates from the sled, tighten the canvas and lashings on them, and use them to help batten down the edges of the tent. All this activity goes on as Scott and Kathleen continue their scene.*)

KATHLEEN. I'm thinking more kindly of you than anyone ever has at any instant of your life. And the price is not small.

SCOTT. How? By letting me run on like a fool?

KATHLEEN. By letting you free. (*She goes to Scott, straightens the scarf around his neck.*) You'll look in on Peter, won't you?

SCOTT. Yes, of course.

KATHLEEN. Oh, we shall form a brave company of two, Master Pedro and I. There's the whole mystery of night time to unravel, and journeys to the park. When I was young — I always wanted so very desperately to have a little boy to play with — if only I could be spared the nuisance of having a husband as well. Well, now you see I shall have my — now I shall have — (*He moves to comfort her, but she pushes him fiercely away.*) No! I will *not* be a silly woman, I *will* not. Now or ever. That much I promise you.

SCOTT. (*Softly.*) I'll come in soon. Just now I have to fix this garden in my mind, every twig, every blade of grass. Just now I have to be alone, love.

KATHLEEN. My poor Con. Will you ever be anything else? (*Scott and Kathleen look at one another in silence.*)

BOWERS. (*Glancing at Scott*) The owner's got a bee in his bonnet over something.

OATES. Nothing new in that.

BOWERS. (*As they continue to work.*) You think you can fathom

25

what he's up to sometimes, and then slam, down it comes over those eyes like steel shutters, and then you might as well be yapping at this bit of canvas.

(*Bowers and Oates glance again at Scott for a moment.*)

OATES. He's close all right. (*Bowers and Oates go back to work. After a moment Kathleen exits. Scott moves slowly* U. *looking at the tent, looking at Oates and Bowers, who ignore him. He examines the entire camp site, then scans the horizon, carefully and critically. He circles the tent, pensively, and goes to the sled, pulling his mittens back on and his balaclava, and straightening the scarf.*)

BOWERS. Hey. How about here, eh? Lovely spot for a picnic? Running water, plenty of shade, bit of a view. I say, hope we shan't be bothered with ants.

OATES. That's even funnier than it was last week, Birdie. And past all comparing to a month ago.

BOWERS. Only trying to look on the bright side.

OATES. You're nothing but sweetness and light the whole day long. It's so depressing.

BOWERS. Guilty of good humour! Never again will I commit so much as a grin. (*Oates spits. Pause. Bowers catches his eye and crosses over to him. They both examine the spot where the spit landed. Bowers spits, experimentally, and they both lean over and cock an ear. Inside the tent Wilson prepares a pot of tea.*) Can't hear the crackle.

OATES. (*Gravely.*) Not quite ready yet. Let's give it a few minutes.

BOWERS. I've always wanted to see spit freeze before it hit the ground. It's been my life's ambition.

OATES. Right. You can't get that in England.

BOWERS. I'm awfully keen on it. (*He spits again and listens critically.*) I think I got one that time! (*Oates shakes his head and moves away.*) You know, Titus, I've been thinking. (*Oates snickers.*) No, no, don't laugh, I can do and have done. And what I've been wondering is—what's the nicest thing you'll remember about Antarctica?

OATES. Leaving it.

BOWERS. Well, that's fair enough, lad, that's well spoke. Not much room for discussion there. (*Pause.*) Are't you going to ask me what I'll remember?

OATES. No, but I've a feeling you're going to tell me. (*At the sled, Scott examines the supply boxes. Bowers sets up a tripod and takes his*

26

chart-book from a pocket. Oates unpacks a surveyor's theodolite and polishes the lens.)

BOWERS. I like the way a day here takes a whole blessed year to go by.

OATES. How do you make that out?

BOWERS. Simple! Logic! It's daylight here for six months, right? A six-month day.

OATES. Right.

BOWERS. And it's night-time here for six months—a six-month night.

OATES. Yes?

BOWERS. Ergo, one day here equals a whole year at home.

OATES. Bra-vo! (*He hands Bowers the theodolite.*)

BOWERS. Scoff all you want, my lad, but this theory of mine explains many puzzling and wondrous things—for instance why the sunrise takes a week here. I don't know whether you noticed, but we had a very lovely dawn last Monday morning through Saturday afternoon. It also explains how we won't seem to grow older as long as we're here—why, blinking takes an hour and a half, and a man may piss for a month! The puzzler is—will it freeze him to the ground?

OATES. We'll be shipping you home in a padded suit, Birdie.

BOWERS. (*Sniffing.*) Good. I'll be warmer that way. (*Bowers sights through the theodolite, marks his chart book. Oates lashes down boxes on the sled, aided by Scott. Inside the tent, Wilson has prepared the pot of tea. Evans is resting, and tries to avoid Wilson's eye.*)

WILSON. Why don't you warm your hands, Eddie?

EVANS. They're fine, Doctor.

WILSON. Still giving you a bit of stiffness?

EVANS. Oh no, I've been rubbing them.

WILSON. You'd tell me if it was otherwise, wouldn't you?

EVANS. Yes sir.

WILSON. There's a good lad. Have some tea. (*Wilson pours a mug and offers it. Evans shakes his head. Wilson sips the tea and watches Evans. Scott takes the sextant from its case on the sled and moves briskly to Bowers.*)

SCOTT. (*Cheerfully.*) Distance, Birdie!

BOWERS. No more than nine miles today. I'm sure of it.

SCOTT. Nine? Where's your pride man? I can't speak for you, but *I* walked eleven-and-a-quarter today!

27

BOWERS. Nothing like eleven! Never eleven.

OATES. (*Grinning at Scott.*) Are we on, then, Birdie?

BOWERS. We're on.

SCOTT. The usual?

BOWERS. As lucky as I feel today? Not likely. Make it two hundred and I'll recoup my losses.

SCOTT. Done.

OATES. Done! We'll clip your wings for you, Birdie.

BOWERS. We'll soon see about that. Nobody in this party has any sense of distance but me — I'm blessed with short legs. (*Bowers puts aside his theodolite and begins to compute their location by sextant, referring repeatedly to the chart book and occasionally working out figures with a pencil. Oates counts the remaining rations, checking totals against a list. Scott takes his little journal and a pencil out of his pocket to record the day's position.*)

SCOTT. (*Writing in his book.*) Monday, January fifteen. The seventy-sixth day of our journey. Oates, what's the mercury?

OATES. (*Glancing at thermometer on side of sled.*) Minus five point seven.

SCOTT. (*Writing.*) Let's hope this warm spell lasts.

OATES. Split the estimates, call it ten miles today. That would leave us — what?

SCOTT. (*Checking figures.*) Only twenty-seven from the Pole.

OATES. So three more marches at this pace! Or two days and a half if we can pick it up!

SCOTT. Four if we should be slowed again . . .

BOWERS. Wilson's with him now. (*A brief pause. They look at one another. Oates glances at the tent.*)

SCOTT. (*To Oates.*) Oates, what's your ration count?

OATES. Fuel for eleven days, food for nine.

SCOTT. The Pole inside of three, and one day there, that's four . . .

OATES. And back to Three Degree Depot in five, or five-and-a-half. Total — nine-and-a-half days. (*Bowers whistles.*)

BOWERS. Cutting it close.

OATES. No! *Easy.* We'll have two biscuits and a teaspoon of parafin for insurance. On the tenth day we shan't eat at all unless we turn up the depot. Birdie will just have to tighten his belt, I suppose.

BOWERS. I don't know why everyone always picks on me. I

work twice as hard as the lot of you. It's only right I should get twice the food.

SCOTT. Bowers, I'm asking you to give up the rest of your lunches for the good of the party. You may chew them on alternate days, but under no circumstances swallow.

BOWERS. Bless you, Captain! A Christian soul . . .

OATES. (*Going to look at Bower's figures.*) How are we doing, then?

BOWERS. (*Still figuring.*) Latitude eight-nine degrees, thirty-three minutes south. Longitude is still—a hundred and sixty—maybe fifty minutes east. Due course, straight for the mark, so that's . . . (*Oates and Scott smile at each other and shake hands.*) Damn! Eleven and one-quarter miles exactly. (*Scott laughs.*) I don't know how he does it.

SCOTT. It's a gift. Shall I add that to your account?

BOWERS. (*Irritated.*) Yes!

SCOTT. (*Writing in his journal.*) That's two thousand, one hundred and sixty-five pounds you owe us, Lieutenant. And don't forget the collateral you put up.

OATES. Your house and mother.

SCOTT. Otherwise we'll *leave* you here.

BOWERS. I'm good for the whole sum! I swear it.

SCOTT. You'd better be. I'm not prepared to win your mother.

BOWERS. She'd rearrange your uppers for that, sir. (*Scott and Oates laugh. Scott sits on a crate, makes another journal entry, and Bowers repositions the theodolite to take a second sighting. Oates sits on the sled. Inside the tent, Wilson still watches Evans.*)

WILSON. What do you make of this, Eddie? (*He takes a small flat stone from his pocket.*) Found it this morning.

EVANS. What is it?

WILSON. (*Turning the stone in his hands.*) A fossil oak leaf.

EVANS. What—here, sir?

WILSON. It seems there were seasons here once, real ones. It was autumn here once, and this leaf fell. As far as you could see, this was all woodland and savannah.

EVANS. Who's she when she's home, sir?

WILSON. (*Smiling.*) It looked like Sussex, Eddie.

EVANS. Think of that! Same leaf as might fall in your own garden. (*Outside the tent, Scott studies the distant horizon.*)

WILSON. Here, have a look. (*With a quick motion, Wilson tosses the stone to Evans who instinctively grabs it with his right hand. As his fingers close around it, Evans cries out softly, and his face distorts with pain. Wilson and Evans stare at one another. Quietly.*) Don't you think you'd better let me see it now?

(*Slowly Evans extends his right hand in his mitten. Wilson places it on his knee, the two of them turning slightly inward towards the stove; we cannot see the hand. We do see Wilson remove the mitten. Evans gives a little gasp. Wilson reacts to the sight of Evan's hand. During the following, Wilson dresses and bandages the wound, taking supplies from his wooden medical kit. Outside the tent, Scott stares with sudden urgency, having seen something in the distance.*)

SCOTT. (*Rising, tensely.*) Oates — the telescope! (*Oates snatches a telescope up from the sled. He and Bowers hurry to Scott's side, the three of them peering off. Bowers climbs on the crate to get a better view.*)

OATES. What is it?

BOWERS. Do you see something?

SCOTT. (*Sighting.*) No. (*Pause.*) A trick of the air, reflecting back our own tent. See it? Hanging there above the horizon, and turned upside down . . .

OATES. Could be a hundred miles, or it could be ten. (*Pause.*) How far ahead do you reckon a real tent could be seen?

BOWERS. I don't know which would be worse — to see them ahead of us, or not to see them at all, but only find their leavings.

OATES. To see them, I think.

BOWERS. In soft powder a dog will bog down same as a man. Amundsen doesn't even know they'll keep pulling for him. Eating each other and the like! Ha! My guess is, he's already turned back. Never seen anything like *this* in his whole life, and wants no part of it.

OATES. (*Grimly.*) Do you want to back that with another two hundred quid?

BOWERS. No. (*Pause.*) Not that one.

OATES. He's got stuff, to take an uncharted route, I'll say that for the bastard. He's got stuff.

BOWERS. You ask me, he's going to hit crevasses with those dogs, same as we have. A man can climb a crevasse where a dog is helpless. Well, what's he to do then, throw them over?

OATES. Perhaps it's smooth where he is — not a crack or hill in sight, only no one ever knew it. Perhaps it's one solid flat sheet of glass. Perhaps he'll skate to the Pole, and be back in time for high tea.

SCOTT. Look out there. (*Pause.*) Can you feel them? Incredible to think—other human beings out there. You strain yours eyes the whole day long, see nothing, hear nothing, still can't believe it somehow—but know it's true. Other warm bodies, hearts pumping blood. That ought to make us feel less lonely, or safer, it seems. Then why is it so shocking? Because—they don't belong here.

OATES. (*Softly.*) Any more than we do.

SCOTT. The possibility of life in this place is more terrifying than the place itself. (*Pause.*) Can it be that we're really here? (*Wilson comes out of the tent, leaving Evans hunched over inside. The others turn to look at him expectantly.*)

WILSON. There's no point mincing words about it. He's got a deep gash on his right palm. From the look of it, he's been hiding it for days. He must have been extraordinarily careful, to keep any of us from seeing it. (*A shocked silence.*)

SCOTT. How deep, Bill?

WILSON. To the bone, or nearly.

OATES. (*After a pause.*) Gangrene?

WILSON. Not yet. It's badly frostbitten, though. The fingers are swollen like sausages. I did the best I could, but he ought to have stiches. (*Pause.*) He ought to have a lot of things.

OATES. (*Letting out a breath.*) Bloody hell.

BOWERS. Christ. No wonder. Poor Taff . . . (*Again there is a silence.*)

SCOTT. Finish stowing this gear. I want a word with him alone.

WILSON. I have some sketches to do. The tea's on.

SCCTT. We'll have hoosh in twenty minutes.

BOWERS. Aye aye, Captain. (*Wilson takes a leather-bound pad from the sled and begins to make sketches of their surroundings, pausing every few moments to blow on his fingers, for he must remove his right mitten to draw. Oates and Bowers pack away the navigational instruments, after which they huddle together on the sled. Oates lights a pipe. Scott goes inside the tent.*)

SCOTT. Hello, Evans

EVANS. (*Nervously.*) Sir. (*He keeps his hand hidden.*)

SCOTT. (*After a pause.*) Tea?

EVANS. Thank you, sir. (*Scott pours him a mug and holds it out. Evans looks at him miserably. Scott holds it up to his lips for him to sip.*) Thank you, sir. Good, that is. (*Scott sits on a crate.*)

SCOTT. Wilson tells me you've had a spot of bad luck.

EVANS. Yes, sir. I'm sorry, sir.

SCOTT. How do you feel?

EVANS. I'm all right now. He put something on it and bandaged me.

SCOTT. I see. (*He pours tea for himself; his hand is shaking badly.*) How did it happen?

EVANS. It was when we shortened the sledge at the depot. It was stupid and careless! I cut my hand on the point of the runner, like a knife it was. After that I — kicked snow over the spots of blood so no-one would see. And later — it began swelling, and it hurt so to keep it in the mitten all the time — I'd slip off the mitten so it didn't burn sometimes — if I was off on point and nobody could see . . .

SCOTT. When was this?

EVANS. (*After a pause.*) Six days ago.

SCOTT. (*Astonished.*) Six? You've been hauling that sled for six days with that hand?

EVANS. Yes, sir.

SCOTT. And yet you never said anything! Never complained.

EVANS. No, sir.

SCOTT. Why, Evans? Why didn't you tell me?

EVANS. (*After a pause.*) It's not so bad now, sir, really it's not. I can close it a little still.

SCOTT. May I see it?

EVANS. You don't want to, Captain. All nasty it is. It's not a proper sight for anybody but me.

SCOTT. May I see it? (*Pause. Evans holds out his partly bandaged hand. We catch a glimpse of the fingers, streaked, vermilion. Scott peels back a piece of gauze. He is stunned despite his efforts to control himself. Quietly.*) Dear God. (*He turns away his face. Evans stares at the ground. Outside the tent, during the above, Oates and Bowers drift to the sled where Wilson sits sketching.*)

OATES. Evans has bought it. He's done us all, more than likely.

BOWERS. We'll all pull for him. Taff will make it.

OATES. And go short rations? *Pull* on short rations?

BOWERS. If we must.

OATES. Evans knows his duty, same as the rest. If he was any sort of man, he'd do what has to be done.

BOWERS. And what's that?

OATES. (*After a pause.*) It's not my place to say.

BOWERS. Over a cut hand?

OATES. (*Angrily.*) Now it's his hand. Next it's his feet, then his legs, then his lights. He'll go to sleep by bits.

BOWERS. Not Taffy!

OATES. Any one of us! There's no point getting sentimental about it, Birdie. It's precious late in the game for that, and the wrong latitude.

WILSON. (*Evenly.*) He's not done yet, not by a mile.

OATES. 'Course he's not! He could hang on for weeks! Eating food the whole time, using fuel the whole time, and slowing us down to a bloody crawl. And then what?

BOWERS. You're a cold-hearted bastard, Oates. You'd tell your mate to do away with himself over a scratch and a portion of biscuit?

OATES. I tell no man anything. But if I were in his place, I'd know what to do.

WILSON. (*Putting down his pad.*) You're not in his place! You can't know what you'd do.

OATES. I'm a soldier, aren't I? And all a soldier needs to know is his duty. We're not one life, we're five. Would you like to kill your mates or kill yourself?

BOWERS. I'd rather live, thank you.

OATES. If it was one or the other?

WILSON. I don't know what I'd do.

OATES. Birdie?

BOWERS. (*Angrily.*) I never thought of it.

OATES. Think of it now. The time may come you'll look at the man walking beside you and hate his guts for not deciding. If it does come, then you've got my opinion already.

BOWERS. You're welcome to it! (*Wilson returns to his sketching. Oates and Bowers are silent and cold, anxious to get inside the tent. Inside, Scott is terribly angry and upset. He has difficulty controlling his voice.*)

SCOTT. Your hand is frostbitten. You know that, don't you? Very badly frostbitten.

EVANS. Well, yes sir. I reckon I did catch a bit of it, didn't I?

SCOTT. Not a bit, a very great deal. If we were back at base camp this hand would be amputated.

EVANS. Well, they might be able to do *something* for me at Base. Stitches and that. I mean, there's always hope, isn't there, sir?

SCOTT. You knew it wouldn't have a chance of healing in this cold. You knew that! And yet you selfishly said nothing. Do you realize what this means to the rest of us?

EVANS. I thought — if I took care of it — it might . . .

SCOTT. (*Furiously.*) Damn it, Evans, stop pretending! Your hand is dead, do you understand that? Dead! It's going to swell up and turn black and rot off your arm!

EVANS. (*Defiantly.*) Yes, *sir.* I knew that right off.

SCOTT. Then why in hell did you keep your mouth shut, you stupid bloody *fool?* (*Scott strikes Evans in the face, Evans recoiling more in shock than pain. Scott looks at his own hand in amazement, then sinks back on his crate. A silence.*)

EVANS. (*Quietly.*) I was afraid you'd send me back. (*Scott is unable to face him.*) I knew you would. One look and you'd've packed me off with the support party, straight back to Base Camp, and I couldn't hardly say I'd blame you. But I didn't want to be sent back, I *couldn't* be sent back — for nothing, for a — a little cut — well that wouldn't have been fair, would it? (*Pause.*) I wanted to go to the Pole. Well, it means a lot to the old ones back in Rhossily that I'd been chosen, look you — and I thought — it'd be worth a hand for that, to go to the Pole, to be one of the first. And so I took my choice, and peace with it. You, you're a wonderful great man, there's babies named after you. That's all I wanted, same as the rest, and I was willing to take my chances right along — I knew I'd never get another my whole life long if I mucked this up. But I never meant to slow you, Captain. God's truth and strike me dead if I did. Please you have to believe that. (*Pause.*) Only, what's to become of me now?

SCOTT. You're going to be all right, Evans. We're all going to pull for you from now on, and that will take the strain off. You can't haul, but you can still march. (*He pours himself another mug of tea.*) You've got to keep your strength up, though. I want you to eat now, and rest.

EVANS. Yes sir. And — you won't send me back?

SCOTT. (*Rising.*) I don't very well see how I can.

EVANS. Oh thank God, sir—thank you! You don't know what this means to me, sir. (*Scott starts to go, then hesitates.*)

SCOTT. Evans—I am very sorry that I raised my voice at you—and that I . . .

EVANS. (*Embarrassedl*) Oh yes, sir. No offense meant, I'm sure, and none taken either.

SCOTT. Thank you, Evans. (*Scott goes outside the tent, still carrying his mug of tea. The others look at him. A momentary silence.*) Hoosh is on, go and eat.

BOWERS. How's Taffy?

SCOTT. Feeling better, I think. Resting.

WILSON. What did he say?

SCOTT. He was afraid of being sent back, it seems. (*Pause.*) In the morning we'll rise a half hour earlier to allow for the extra time it takes him. On the march, we'll alternate taking his turn pulling. I'll take three turns to every other man's two, and he'll bring up the rear. I'm cutting the food and fuel rations per man beginning at breakfast. Questions?

WILSON. Clear enough.

BOWERS. Fine.

SCOTT. Oates?

OATES. (*After a pause.*) Yes, sir.

SCOTT. Rise is at five-thirty then. (*He moves away from the tent. Oates and Bowers enter the tent. Wilson pauses near Scott.*)

WILSON. Robert, I should have . . .

SCOTT. No, Bill.

WILSON. I had suspicions.

SCOTT. We all did. My fault. Go and eat. (*Wilson goes into the tent with the others. They crowd round the stove. There's a moment of tension with Evans, who shrinks away and avoids their eyes. This tension is broken when Bowers pats his shoulder. Wilson begins to dish out mugs of stew; they mumur quietly among themselves, eating. Lights fade slowly on the tent area, and u. generally. There is the sound of the wind again, louder than before. As Wilson goes into the tent, Amundsen appears suddenly. Scott is startled.*)

AMUNDSEN. Give us some tea. My blood's turned to ice. (*Scott stares at him. Amundsen goes and takes the mug from Scott, then drinks gratefully.*) Christ that's good. (*He drinks again.*) That line of clouds, you've seen them?

SCOTT. (*Looking out.*) Yes.

AMUNDSEN. Stormheads. But too early for this season. I've never seen such clouds.

SCOTT. Yes . . .

AMUNDSEN. Well, we can't think of everything. Between the far edge of the plan and the near edge of danger, there's always just that tiny crack of luck. So narrow you could barely drive a man's hand into it. (*He sips again.*)

SCOTT. He had no right to keep it to himself. It doesn't make any sense!

AMUNDSEN. Why should it? This cold—so hard on a sick man. He never heals.

SCOTT. First frostbite, then gangrene.

AMUNDSEN. Snow blindness.

SCOTT. Exhaustion . . .

AMUNDSEN. Madness. (*Pause.*) Really, it's an extraordinary place. It wants so much for you to be dead.

SCOTT. I struck him! I can't believe I struck him.

AMUNDSEN. He behaved like a fool.

SCOTT. But I had no right! A sick man, and a petty officer at that . . .

AMUNDSEN. Which bothers you more—that you struck him, or that he's going to die? (*Scott looks at Amundsen steadily.*) Toughen your heart, English. You know what has to be done.

SCOTT. Yes. I must leave him behind . . .

AMUNDSEN. Of course.

SCOTT. Not—when he's still walking, not tomorrow or the next day, but soon . . .

AMUNDSEN. Easier for him than for you. Maybe he won't wake at all.

SCOTT. The others slipping away before dawn . . .

AMUNDSEN. He's rolled warm in his sleeping-bag. He doesn't hear or see. He feels nothing.

SCOTT. He wakes at noon. The silent tent. The empty miles around.

AMUNDSEN. But the others saved.

SCOTT. One lost, but the others saved. And peace for him...

AMUNDSEN. (*Taking a flask from his coat.*) It must be done.

SCOTT. Yes. It must . . .

AMUNDSEN. And I want to do it. (*He pours from this flask into Scott's mug.*)

SCOTT. And I want to . . .

AMUNDSEN. For myself. For my own sake.

SCOTT. Yes. (*Self-disgustedly.*) For my own sake. (*Amundsen hands the mug to Scott, who drinks.*)

AMUNDSEN. Well. Where's it written that a general should stop a bullet for a private? That's against all rules of strategy. He's finally only a common sort of oaf—too clumsy even to avoid spearing himself.

SCOTT. (*Lost in himself.*) What? (*Amundsen caps the flask and returns it to his coat.*)

AMUNDSEN. One sick man is sacrificed for the good of the many. Don't worry, there's no danger of any stain on your reputation. You might even seem a greater hero than ever.

SCOTT. You disgust me.

AMUNDSEN. For speaking common sense! You're thinking a miracle will come along.

SCOTT. It's still only his hand! He just needn't haul any more.

AMUNDSEN. And when he can no longer walk? What then?

SCOTT. Then we'll put him on the sled and drag him.

AMUNDSEN. For God's sake, English! (*He picks up a large crate.*) The sled weighs one thousand pounds already. (*He heaves the crate on to the sled.*) Now! The weight of a big man! If not for your ridiculous pride you might have dogs drag it, instead of cripples! And when he slows you down so much you can't reach your supplies—will you drag him even then?

SCOTT. If we must.

AMUNDSEN. He is one. You are four.

SCOTT. That makes no difference.

AMUNDSEN. The difference between living and dying!

SCOTT. Should I just shoot him then, like one of your dogs? Damn it, perhaps we could eat him as well—just to be absolutely logical! It's my fault he's here. Can't you see I'm responsible for his life?

AMUNDSEN. (*Furiously.*) For many lives! There's one way to live here, one only! Everything is a *tool*—a boot, a sled, a dog—and a hand, an arm, even a man! If it breaks down you throw it away and you march on! It's brutal, yes! And it's ugly. But anything else is sentiment and it will kill you!

SCOTT. There's a wall. I can see myself approaching from a great distance—and at last I come to it. On this side I'm something like myself. On the other side I'm lost, I have no name. (*Pause.*) Can't you understand? Where is the point at which the entire thing becomes worthless? After one man dies? After two?

AMUNDSEN. Then turn back now. (*Scott stares at him, then turns away.*) No, I never thought you would. Easier to wait. Easier not to decide. (*Facing the tent, Amundsen claps his hands twice, sharply. Scott's men immediately stir and begin to silently break camp and load the supplies and tent on to the sled. When they have completed packing, Evans slips off R.. The others pull the sled far L., then stop and turn back facing R.. They remain stationary until the beginning of the next scene, as if having halted in their march. Amundsen walks away from Scott and looks again at the sky.*) God, these winds. They come across five thousand miles, nothing to interest or slow them up along the way, for the simple pleasure of burning my face.

SCOTT. I have one duty to the nation. Another to these men. Are they no longer the same?

AMUNDSEN. You have a selfish ambition as well.

SCOTT. (*After a pause.*) God help me. I don't know any longer which I place the highest.

AMUNDSEN. Duty. Honour. Sacrifice. All very nice on a full belly.

SCOTT. But what is a leader, if he can't locate his duty above his own ambition?

AMUNDSEN. A man, such as other men. He outshines the angels, he kills his brother for a scrap of bread. Oh yes, English, you will too when your time comes.

SCOTT. I am not capable. If I were—I shouldn't want to live myself.

AMUNDSEN. English, you don't even know who you are. You've learned every single rule, but not one dark corner of your own heart. You're the most dangerous kind of decent man.

BOWERS. (*Shouting off toward R.*) Evans!

AMUNDSEN. Think of the fox, with his leg caught in a steel trap. He'll gnaw through his own flesh for the chance to save his life.

OATES. (*Shouting.*) Evans!

AMUNDSEN. (*Taking the flask again from his coat.*) *Become* the fox—feel the metal grinding into bone, smell your own hot blood running—and then ask yourself which it is you really love most: the leg—or the trap? (*Amundsen slips the flask into Scott's hands and exits. Scott turns as he does so.*)

OATES. Evans, damn you!

SCOTT. *EVANS!*

WILSON. No use, we'll just have to wait again.

OATES. He'll never keep up, that one. He's too weak.

BOWERS. I'm going back.

SCOTT. No! Let him come as quickly as he can.

BOWERS. If I just give him a hand . . .

SCOTT. I don't want him feeling helpless. I don't want him pitying himself. Sooner or later we're going to have to carry him, but for now let him do his best. (*Scott hands the flask to Bowers. Wilson, kneeling at the rear of the sled, checks the mileage on their odometer. The wind fades away.*)

WILSON. (*Excitedly.*) Do you realize—we've done almost nine miles already! In one morning.

BOWERS. Eighteen more! That's . . .

WILSON. That's tomorrow noon! (*Wilson and Bowers laugh and hug in excitement, slapping each other's back. Oates limps to the sled and sits.*)

OATES. Oh Christ, my legs are on fire . . .

BOWERS. My whole corpse is. (*He drinks from the flask.*)

SCOTT. Are you all right, Bowers?

BOWERS. Pink! Pink! That's what I'm in. I'm in the bleeding pink. (*He passes the flask to Wilson.*)

WILSON. I don't know how you manage to keep up, with those tiny little legs. (*He drinks, then passes the flask to Oates.*)

SCOTT. By taking two steps to our one.

BOWERS. The Owner's right. I've walked twice as far as the ruddy lot of you. (*Oates drinks.*)

OATES. Lord, that's good.

BOWERS. Getting colder.

WILSON. It may have dropped off three or four degrees.

OATES. What difference does it make? I've got nothing left to freeze but my ballocks, and no use for them. (*He drinks again.*)

SCOTT. How's that hip, Oates?

OATES. (*Rubbing.*) Bit stiff.

WILSON. Watch you don't cramp.

BOWERS. Oh, that's all we need. Soldier and his gamey hip.

WILSON. Birdie! A little respect, if you please, for our walking wounded. (*He kneels by Oates to rub his leg.*)

OATES. Here, Birdie, he's right. You're talking to a blessed war hero. Saved East Grinstead from the dreaded Boer menace. (*The others laugh. Oates drinks again.*)

BOWERS. Some hero. You got that hip in a knocking-shop in Capetown.

OATES. (*With mock dignity.*) My dear chap, I was nobly bled on the glorious field of honour.

BOWERS. Oh go on, Titus, pull the other one. Shot in the bum by some poor woman's husband, more like. (*They laugh.*)

OATES. There I was, alone in the Transvaal, facing fifty of the brutes . . .

WILSON. Oh make it a hundred.

OATES. All right, fifty in front, fifty behind.

SCOTT. Oh dear. (*They laugh.*)

OATES. My regiment called back, or mostly dead, and me left with a bullet in the hip . . .

BOWERS. And one in the head, too, I should think. (*They laugh.*)

OATES. There's old Titus, and not a stick of shade for fifty yards. It was a hundred degrees, the flies came like smoke. (*Pause. The others fall very silent.*) And so—for ten hours, my leg like—raspberry jam, hip to kneecap. (*He laughs.*) Thighbone shattered—just here—and the sun. Please God let there be a bullet left in my pouch, just one—no bullet. Then my soul for a mouthful of spit. No spit. But the flies. And the sun and the sun . . . (*Pause.*) And so I says to myself, Titus, me lad, if you should pull through, it's good-bye to the tropic climes. Promise me you'll put in for a cooler line of work—Antarctica!

WILSON
BOWERS } "That's the place for you!" } (*Shouting together.*)
OATES

(*They all laugh. Evans staggers on* R.*. He is panting, his chest heaves. The others turn, startled.*)

EVANS. Why-why-ve—you stopped? (*His legs buckle, he starts to collapse. Wilson and Bowers are the first to reach him.*)

BOWERS. Easy, Taffy!

40

SCOTT. Pick him up. On the sledge.

WILSON. Oates, the legs. Birdie help. Everyone rubbing him.

EVANS. (*Protesting weakly.*) All right — I'm all right . . .

WILSON. Keep still. (*They lay Evans out flat on the sled.*)

EVANS. Just need get breath . . .

WILSON. (*Taking the flask from Oates and holding it to Evan's mouth.*) Drink. (*Evans drinks, chokes.*)

BOWERS. Easy.

EVANS. (*Trying to rise.*) No more.

WILSON. A swallow.

SCOTT. Just to get your wind back.

EVANS. Sorry. Don't know what — happened me back there.

WILSON. (*Putting the flask in his pocket.*) It's all right, Eddie, you've just had a bit of slow going, that's all.

EVANS. Feet kept sticking in snow. Couldn't lift. (*He tries to rise.*) Won't happen again.

SCOTT. Rest. Don't try to move.

EVANS. How — how far?

SCOTT. We've done nine miles today.

EVANS. (*Shaking his head.*) How far to the Pole?

SCOTT. Eighteen.

EVANS. Be there tomorrow!

BOWERS. That's right, Taff.

OATES. His legs are like wood.

WILSON. He's getting cramped. When he's caught his breath help him up. I want him walking.

EVANS. Better now. Kept us here long enough. Let me up. (*They restrain him again.*) Please!

WILSON. (*Nodding to Scott.*) Slowly then. Help him, Birdie. Take his arm. (*Wilson and Bowers support Evans, one under each arm. They walk him back and forth slowly.*)

BOWERS. How're the old pins, eh? Holding steady, are they?

EVANS. (*Weakly.*) Yes.

BOWERS. All you need, Taffy, is a bit of a tune. Sing him one, Soldier.

OATES. I don't know what to sing.

BOWERS. Well, I do. What do you say, Taff — a Welsh song, eh?

EVANS. Yes . . .

BOWERS. You know this one. (*He sings.*) "Men of Harlech,

march to glo-ry . . . " Come on, Eddie, sing with me—"Victory is hov'ring o'er ye . . . " Come on!

EVANS. Yes . . .

BOWERS. (*Singing.*) "Bright-eyed freedom stands before ye—Hear ye not her call?" (*Scott and Wilson join in with the song, and then Oates as well. They march Evans back and forth jauntily, in rhythm with the music. Towards the end Evans joins in weakly. They sing out boisterously, as if almost drunk with this release of tension.*)

All (*singing.*)

Echoes loudly waking,
Hill and valley shaking,
Till the sound spreads wide around,
The saxon's courage breaking!

Upon their soil we never sought them—
Love of conquest hither brought them,
But this lesson we have taught them—
Cambria ne'er can yield!

(*During the last stanza the song trails off as one by one they become aware that Evans has stopped singing. He is staring at something on the ground, down far* L. *and off. He breaks from Wilson and Bowers and hobbles slowly across, stands for a moment looking out, then slumps to his knees. Bowers is the last to stop singing. He looks around. Long pause, as they filter towards the kneeling Evans.*)

SCOTT. (*Softly*) What is it, Evans? What's wrong?

EVANS. (*Staring with childlike wonder.*) Tracks. Of dogs. (*They all stare out and down, motionless. The sound of the wind is heard. The lights shift abruptly, as if the sun was wheeling across the sky with impossible speed. Amundsen enters* U. *He carries a bamboo pole. A small Norwegian flag is attached to the top of this, and a leather pouch to its bottom. He plants this pole up* C. *and kneels for a moment, looking up at the flag. He gets to his feet again, moves* R. *and stops. He watches Scott. Scott and his men turn slowly and look at the flag. They fan out silently and slowly into a random pattern across the stage, first looking at the flag but not approaching it, and then looking anywhere else but at the flag. There is an agonized silence. Evans kneels to one side and picks at the ground. At last Scott walks to the flag, kneels at its base, pulls open the leather pouch. He takes a letter from inside.*)

SCOTT. (*Reading aloud, barely a whisper.*) "Roald Amundsen. Olav Bjaaland. Hilmer Hanssen . . ."

AMUNDSEN. "Sverre Hassel. Oscar Wisting. Sixteenth December, nineteen eleven."

SCOTT. "Captain Scott . . . " (*His voice falters.*)

AMUNDSEN. "Captain Scott. Will you be so good as to forward these effects at the earliest possible date . . . "

SCOTT. "Along with the enclosed letters, to His Majesty King Haakon the Seventh of Norway. I am sure you can appreciate their importance — as corroboration of what has happened."

AMUNDSEN. "Please believe that for your sake I am as truly sorry as it is possible to be —"

SCOTT. " — at such a moment . . . " (*Scott's hand drifts down with the letter. Bowers takes the letter from him, reads further. Amundsen turns and goes.*)

OATES. (*Feverishly.*) Birdie, take a sighting. They've made a mistake. (*He scrambles to the sled and gets the sextant.*)

BOWERS. (*Quietly,*) There's no mistake.

OATES. Damn it, you can't know without checking! Take a sighting — here!

BOWERS. (*Holding out the letter.*) There's no mistake. They were here for three days.

OATES. (*Striking down the letter.*) Take a sighting!

BOWERS. They cross-checked from different co-ordinates!

OATES. (*Raging.*) They could've been off! They could've been off a hundred yards! You said yourself it's never precise. We could still be the first at the exact spot!

BOWERS. (*Angrily.*) Titus, for God's sake — it doesn't matter! One yard, ten — they were *here!*

OATES. Well, I don't believe it! Hell! Bloody stinking *hell!* (*He raises the sextant above his head.*)

BOWERS. (*Shouting.*) Titus — no! (*Oates controls himself with an effort and lowers the sextant. Bowers takes it from him and carries it back to the sled.*)

WILSON. (*Turning.*) North — north in every direction. Think of that. (*Pause.*) Strange that it's no different, really, from any other . . . I mean somehow I'd hoped — perhaps it might . . . (*Pause.*) Childish, I suppose.

EVANS. (*Still kneeling.*) Well, we got here. That's something, isn't it? I mean we did get here, eight hundred miles on foot. Anyway — we might beat them back with the news. We could say we got here first and they're lying. Who's to know the difference? (*Oates turns to stare at Evans.*)

BOWERS. Not likely we'd beat them back. They've a month's head start — and missed the worst weather.

OATES. This is *your* bloody fault, Evans. Do you hear me?

SCOTT. Belay that, Mr. Oates.

OATES. How do you like this nice piece of work you — (*Moving to Evans.*) — weakling, you bloody pathetic liar — and coward!

SCOTT. I said enough!

OATES. Well, let me shake your hand on it! (*Oates squeezes Evan's crippled hand. Evans screams. Bowers leaps at Oates's back, spins him away from Evans, smashes him across the face. Evans falls. Oates is knocked to the ground. He tries to come back at Evans again, but Scott and Bowers restrain him. Evans rolls away. He lies huddled and crying, nursing his hand. Oates, in his dazed fury, still curses Evans incoherently.*) You great — you — oh God — you just wait, Evans — you see if I don't get you for this . . .

BOWERS. (*Gently.*) Titus — we missed them by a whole month. I suppose we never really . . . (*He glances at Scott.*) What I'm trying to say is — it didn't really make that much difference. It's not his fault, Titus. (*A long silence. Evans sobs softly.*)

WILSON. Gentlemen. I've one last cigar that I'd been saving for this day. I've always wanted to see this place, since I was a boy, and now I'm here, and I'm not sorry for it. (*Pause.*) And I say, to hell with the Norskers, I'm going to smoke it anyway. (*He lights the cigar and puffs.*)

BOWERS. (*Managing a grin.*) How is it?

WILSON. (*Sadly.*) I've had better. (*He passes the cigar to Bowers.*)

SCOTT. (*Briskly.*) Right, then! (*He takes a small British flag from his parka.*) Oates, I think perhaps our little Union Jack might present a braver apperance than that bit of rag. Just tie it there. (*He gives the flag to Oates.*) We'll be having hoosh here as quickly as you and Evans can get it made. You'll be working on that detail together, please, and you may break open that last tin of plum pudding. Bowers, please set up the Kodak.

BOWERS. (*Surprised.*) You want the camera, sir?

SCOTT. We're at the Pole! I think we owe history a photograph of that, don't you? I want that at once, Bowers, first thing.

BOWERS. Aye, aye, Captain. (*Bowers crosses to the sled and finds the camera in one of the chests. He props it up on the ground down* C., *at-taching a long string to the shutter so he can include himself in the picture. Oates pulls down the Norwegian flag and attaches the Union Jack to the pole.*)

SCOTT. (*To Wilson.*) Bill, make whatever sketches you need as quickly as you can. We leave as soon as we're rested. (*He moves back to Oates. The men begin to move into position for a photograph* C., *facing out front. They move sluggishly at first, but Scott tries to galvanize them with his energy.*) Very good, Oates. Now help me give Evans a hand up, will you, and let's just brush him down. Come on Evans, on your feet, man. (*Oates and Scott help Evans to his feet and brush him down.*) Bowers, are you ready for us there?

BOWERS. Nearly, sir.

SCOTT. Right then. Bill, let's see — I'll ask you to sit in front, and Bowers, you're so damned short you'll *have* to sit in front, or we shan't be able to see you at all — and then how will we prove to your mother you were even here? Oates, over there, and Evans, I think perhaps if you'll stand with me we can make a reasonable sort of back row — that's the idea — splendid!

(*They settle into a tableau, posed for the photograph. Bowers and Wilson sit in front, Oates, Scott and Evans standing behind them. The lights fade quickly, so that Scott and his men are in silhouette, with only a soft front light. The sound of the wind becomes slightly louder. Kathleen enters as the stage goes mainly dark and a spot comes up on her.*)

KATHLEEN. My dearest Con, I am determined to write each diary entry as though I spoke to you directly, for I know it will make me feel closer to you. (*Pause.*) Tomorrow will be our wedding day. We shall have been married three years. I bet anything you won't remember it. (*Pause.*) I thought of you last night when I walked along the beach, down to where you and I once went. You know the place, right along where the river flows into the sea. I saw the very tuft of grass that we sat upon. It was more beautiful today than then, for there was an exquisite sunset over the marshes, the moon was rising, and not a sound but by my bare toes on the wet sand. I wanted you more than I have done for long and long. I wonder — if you will be here with me by the spring. (*The spot softens but does not fade completely on Kathleen. A second spot picks Scott out of the group of men posed* C.)

SCOTT. Oh little girl, I do think of you now. (*Pause.*) You used to joke about how I was always late for dinner parties — every time I had an important engagement the train or bus would break down, and I'd miss something that might've made all the difference. Well, it's never been the right time for me, Kath. I feel — I feel like some ludicrous footnote to history — and I had so hoped for better things. Now it's good-bye to the daydreams, and eight hundred miles to march home. At least — there's a kind of relief to finally be certain of something. A man unburdened by hope is like a god, or a machine. He never tires, or feels sorry for himself, never feels afraid — or anything at all. (*With a terrible cry.*) But Great God! This is an awful place! And it's terrible enough to have come here, without the reward of priority! (*Kathleen turns, watching Scott. The wind rises.*)

BOWERS. (*Quietly.*) Ready, sir.

SCOTT. I shan't expect any man to smile. But I would take it as a favour if no man looked as though he were beaten.

BOWERS. Whenever you say.

SCOTT. Then I say now. (*Bowers pulls the string. There is a flash and a puff of smoke from the camera. The lights brighten for a long moment with terrible intensity on the rigid little group. They hold very bright for perhaps a count of five. Brisk, martial-sounding band music comes in and builds. Amundsen enters and joins into the pose, putting his arms around the shoulders of Scott and Evans, and turning to smile out at the audience. Very suddenly all lights snap to black, and the wind fades abruptly. Above, a massive image appears — a photograph of the actual party posed at the Pole, as they are represented below by the actors on the stage. Amundsen, of course, is not in the slide. The actors exit in the light of this slide, which holds. The music continues as the house lights rise for the Intermission.*)

ACT II

Darkness and silence. Pause, then a waltz is played softly.
A series of slides appears, as at the start of Act I.
The first slide is a photograph of young Prince Edward, wear-
ing a top hat and smoking a cigar at a jaunty angle.
A street scene in Edwardian London. Men in bowler hats and
holding canes, women in long dresses, wide-brimmed hats, and
parasols. The sidewalks are crowded, as well as the street,
which bustles with both horse-drawn carriages and automobiles.
Elegant men and women at a lawn party. The women hold cro-
quet mallets. All smile and squint at the camera, peering into
bright sunlight.
A group of spectators at the Henley Regatta. Sunlight sparkling
off water, and flowers.
Edwardian children at play. The girls wear ruffled skirts, and
the boys, knickers.
A nanny with two little girls and a pram in a municipal park.
An elegant restaurant, crowded with diners. There are potted
palms and long, gilt-framed mirrors.
King Edward VII as an old and stout man, sitting in a chair.
His hair and beard are white, his face appears racked with sick-
ness. A crowd of people standing on a dock watching a three-
masted steamship being towed in for mooring. A tug is pulling
the ship towards the dock.
Though we have no way of seeing such details, the ship is the
Terra Nova, and the people are in mourning.
The last slide holds as the first stage light comes up — a strange
sparkling, ten feet above stage level c. — tiny, mysterious flashes
of light. These resolve into a beautiful chandelier, crystals dangl-
ing like icicles. The scrim lights up, dissolving the slide, and in
silhouette light we can see an elegant dining table, surrounded by
five chairs. It is laid with formal place settings — there are wine
glasses, and a lovely floral arrangement in the middle. Around
this tableau the setting remains unchanged from Act I.

*The music continues as Scott, Wilson, Evans, and Oates enter
from different directions. They greet one another in silhouette.
There is ad lib. joking and laughter, murmured conversation.
They seem to be seeing one another for the first time in a great
while, and renewing acquaintances. As they sit at the table up
c. the lights rise on them. They are all in formal evening dress.
Bowers, also in evening dress, enters as the others sit.
The waltz music continues throughout the following scene, until
a stop is indicated.*

OATES. (*To Bowers.*) Well?
BOWERS. (*Seating himself.*) That bugger had the bloody cheek
to think he could palm off an eighteen ninety-five Château-
Pissoir on us, but I told the wretched fellow it was vinegar, pure
vinegar, and that he'd best look sharp or he'd lose our custom.
OATES. Stout fellow!
WILSON. Did you manage a look at their cellar?
BOWERS. Mmm. They've a lovely little eighty-seven
Bordello. He pleaded with me to accept that instead, com-
pliments of the *maison,* so I told him I might — just *might,* mind
you, but I couldn't *promise* — be able to talk you into considering
it. What do you say?
OATES. An eighty-seven Bordeau? Well, I don't know . . .
WILSON. Oh come on, Soldier! There's no point in hurting
their feelings.
BOWERS. We'll *pretend* that it's drinkable.
SCOTT. (*Sighing.*) Otherwise we'll be here all night.
OATES. Oh very well. But I wish to God someone would explain to me how a *Bordeaux* is supposed to sit with my *fondue de
poulet.*
WILSON. There's a good fellow. We can always switch with
the next course.
(*A waiter enters, in uniform. It is Amundsen. He goes to the head of the
table, where Scott is sitting.*)
AMUNDSEN. (*In a French accent.*) M'sieu is ready to order
now?
SCOTT. Thank you, yes. Let's see. (*He picks up a menu from the
table. Scott's spoken French is fair, Wilson's is quite good, that of the
others is atrocious.*) I'll have the *poulet rôti à la Normande.* That's
with the giblet and herb stuffing, is it?

48

AMUNDSEN. *Oui, çest ca.*

SCOTT. Perhaps a green salad might do nicely as well. Is the lettuce fresh?

AMUNDSEN. *Mais certainement, m'sieu.*

SCOTT. Quite fresh?

AMUNDSEN. It is very crisp.

SCOTT. Very well, a green salad. Birdie?

BOWERS. Right, I've been looking forward to this for eons. I'll have the *tournedos sautés aux champignons.*

AMUNDSEN. *Oui, m'sieu.* (*He turns, moving to Oates.*)

BOWERS. Wait a minute Froggy, I'm not finished. (*Amundsen turns back.*) *Jambon farci en croûte. Champignons sautés à la crème. Carrottes glacées. Rognons de veau flambés . . .*

SCOTT. For God's sake, Birdie, don't be such a pig.

BOWERS. I'm *starvin'!* I'm so peckish I could bite my own *leg* off! — (*He gestures to Amundsen.*) — or anyway, his leg. (*To Amundsen, politely.*) And some of those nice Italian truffles, if you please.

AMUNDSEN. As *M'sieu* wishes. (*He turns to Oates.*) *M'sieu?*

OATES. *Fondue poulet à la crème,* please, and Beluga Malassol Caviar. You do *have* the Malassol? Because I'm not interested in any of your Turkish sediment.

AMUNDSEN. Fresh this morning, m'sieu. I inspect the shipment personally.

OATES. Good lad. Doctor?

WILSON. Just the *filets de poisson Bercy aux champignons, s'il vous plaît.* Nothing too heavy for me.

SCOTT. Come come, Bill, you can put away more than that!

WILSON. No, really, the old stomach's feeling a bit offish.

SCOTT. Evans?

EVANS. (*After a pause, peering at his menu.*) I can't quite make this out.

OATES. (*Leaning over.*) Where are you looking? Oh, there. "Jules Roussin, *Maitre Chef.*" (*Grinning.*) Mmm, that sounds delicious!

EVANS. Yes, that sounds good. I'll have some of that.

WILSON. Oh for God's sake, Edgar, you just ordered the head cook! (*They all laugh; Evans is embarrassed.*)

BOWERS. (*To Amundsen.*) We'll have him skewered, please, lightly marinated in butter and lemon juice, and served *flambée.*

49

SCOTT. Evans will have the braised duck with chestnut and sausage stuffing. (*Gently.*) Is that all right, Evans?

EVANS. Yes sir. That sounds fine.

SCOTT. Good. That's all, waiter. We'll order the other courses separately. You may bring along the wine.

AMUNDSEN. *Oui, m'sieu, immediatement!* (*Amundsen bows and exits.*)

WILSON. Dicey-lookin' fella.

OATES. The service here's appalling.

BOWERS. (*With a shrug.*) He's a foreigner, what did you expect?

OATES. Right. Shoot them all!

EVANS. (*Lifting a glass, shyly.*) I propose a toast.

WILSON. We don't have any wine yet!

EVANS. Oh—well. (*Pause; a bit doubtfully.*) I propose a toast with water, then.

OATES. (*To Wilson.*) Is that on? (*Wilson shrugs.*)

BOWERS. Speak up, Taffy!

OATES. And stand up! You're supposed to stand. (*Evans rises shyly, lifts his glass. He notices that his napkin is stuffed in his waistband, pulls it out and drops it on the table, then lifts his glass again.*)

EVANS. To Captain Scott—the truest and finest officer that a sailor could ever ask to ship under.

BOWERS. Hear hear.

EVANS. He never asked us to do anything he wouldn't do himself—and if he ever finds himself another place he hasn't been to—I'll be the first to sign aboard. (*Pause.*) That's all I wanted to say.

SCOTT. (*Touched.*) Thank you, Evans. (*Bowers, Oates and Wilson stand.*)

WILSON. (*Raising his glass.*) Hear hear!

SCOTT. (*Rising.*) We really ought to drink first to His Majesty. Gentlemen—I give you the King.

ALL. The King! (*They toast and "drink."*)

BOWERS. God save him.

OATES. (*Quietly.*) And thanks be to God for a safe return to our families.

WILSON. Amen.

BOWERS. Yes! To our sweethearts and wives—may they never meet! (*They sit, laughing and "drinking."*)

OATES. (*Tapping on his glass.*) Speech!

BOWERS. Yes! The Owner's got to make a speech!

SCOTT. No . . . (*All of them exclaim enthusiastically, "Speech!"—"Yes, speech!", etc. Scott remains standing while the others settle back in thier seats.*) I'm not going to come to any more of these reunions if you're going to make me get up and lecture. (*They laugh.*) I can see us in twenty years, a pack of wrinkled old fools boasting into each other's ear trumpets about the things we never even did. (*They laugh.*) We've come through a lot together. I want you to know that I was very pleased with each one of you, with your dedication and sacrifice, not just to our mission, but to me personally as well. (*Pause.*) None of you had to go south. Each of you volunteered, at great personal hazard, leaving behind families and loved ones. I'm sorry that we didn't reach the Pole first—but I will never be sorry for the way we tried—and you shouldn't be either. Ignore the detractors—be just one-tenth as proud of your efforts as I have been—and what we've accomplished can never seem a failure, or an empty gesture. (*Pause.*) Something that I could never say, somehow, during the course of our journey, and that is difficult for me to express, even now—but nonetheless true for all that: I love you each as if you were my own sons. (*Pause.*) I suppose that's my real speech. (*Pause.*) Now for God's sake let's get on with the food.

(*A momentary silence.*)

BOWERS. (*Enthusiastically, jumping to his feet.*) Three cheers for the Old Man!

(*They give three boisterous cheers, followed by ad lib. laughter and congratulations as the waltz music swells. Amidst the hubbub Amundsen enters quietly, unnoticed, and stands to one side. He has taken off the waiter's outfit and now waits silently, ominously, in his own coat. With Amundsen's entrance, the waltz music very abruptly stops. After a moment of silence, we hear the sound of the wind. Slowly and in puzzlement Scott and his men turn, reacting to Amundsen's presence and the wind. One or two of them slowly sink back into their chairs as they see him.*)

AMUNDSEN. (*Simply.*) There is no food.

SCOTT. What? (*After a pause; stunned.*) No roast chicken? No green salad?

WILSON. No fish in wine sauce with mushrooms . . .

(*Amundsen watches them silently. u., playing over the scrim, the beginnings of a strange lighting effect. Pale, eerie streaks of red and lavender*) *and green tumble and shift across the cyclorama, in ghostly vertical slashes. The chandelier is flown out, slowly.*)

SCOTT. Yes. Well. (*Pause.*) Perhaps we'd better be going, then.

OATES. (*Dazed.*) Perhaps another time.

BOWERS. Right, then. Well, I'm not really surprised.

(*Bowers, Evans, Wilson and Oates leave silently, filing off in different directions. They carry their chairs with them as they shuffle away. Bowers takes Scott's chair as well as his own. Scott stands* C. *Amundsen moves to the table and turns up the edge of the tablecloth, which has been trailing along the floor, and then puts it on the tabletop. As he lifts the cloth we see that the "table" all along has actually been the sled. Scott moves down* C., *facing out front, as Amundsen continues piling the edges of the tablecloth over the center of the sled, pushing the floral arrangement and place settings into a heap.*)

AMUNDSEN. How do you like your game now, English? Where will you find the rules?

SCOTT. In myself.

AMUNDSEN. That's a large enough space to explore.

SCOTT. It's all you've left me.

AMUNDSEN. No proud speeches now? (*Pause.*) You disappoint me, English, you've changed. You've softened.

SCOTT. No. On the contrary.

AMUNDSEN. I am always with you now. You and I are married together now, like one person. We have both been to the Pole. (*Amundsen takes Scott's Antarctic parka out of the sled. His scarf, mittens, and other gear are in the pockets of this coat. Amundsen moves behind Scott. During the following he helps Scott off with his evening jacket, and helps him on with the arctic gear.*)

SCOTT. (*Looking out front, fascinated.*) Those strange colors . . .

AMUNDSEN. Yes. The Aurora Australis.

SCOTT. Of course, the Southern Lights. (*Pause.*) I've always wondered what they must be like.

AMUNDSEN. Radiant energy released in the high atmosphere. They almost seem to sway with the breezes. Very beautiful, aren't they?

SCOTT. Flames exploding in air. Colors falling from the sky . . .

AMUNDSEN. Form, color, movement — mysterious and brief as life. We used to watch the Northern Lights as children. To

52

me these are far more awesome. (*Wilson, Bowers and Oates enter;*
they are dressed now in their Antarctic clothes. They cross slowly and
painfully to the sled and pick up their leather traces.) The ancients, you
know, considered these lights to be mystic signs and portents.
SCOTT. "The fiery handwriting of the gods."
WILSON. (*To Scott.*) Robert, are you all right?
SCOTT. (*Still looking.*) All right, yes.
WILSON. Are you coming?
SCOTT. I'm coming . . . (*Wilson exchanges a worried glance with*
Bowers. He motions that they should go ahead. Wilson, Bowers and
Oates exit with the sled, Wilson looking back over his shoulder at Scott.
To Amundsen) Did they—consider them good luck, or bad?
AMUNDSEN. Well. I suppose that depends whether you were
an ancient optimist, or an ancient pessimist.
SCOTT. Then how should we consider them?
AMUNDSEN. Ah. We of course must pretend to be modern
men, with no time for such gaudy superstitions. (*Evans enters,*
trailing well behind the others. He crosses the stage with great difficulty,
one foot dragging, his head down.) But they remind me that we live
on a very small planet, and will never have the answers to some
questions. For instance the question—what is it that keeps this
man walking? (*Scott turns, just in time to see Evans drop to his knees,*
breathing deeply and staring straight ahead.)
SCOTT. (*Alarmed.*) Evans . . . !
AMUNDSEN. Look at him.
(*Scott goes and crouches beside the unseeing Evans, and looks into his*
face.)
His hands are swollen to lumps. The fingernails are all dis-
lodged. Fluid streams constantly down his legs and freezes there
in seconds. (*He goes to Scott and Evans.*) His ears are lost, the tip
of the nose. The mind is clouded, dull, stupid. (*Pause.*) Then
how is it this creature is still able to put one foot in front of the
other?
SCOTT. (*Softly.*) Home.
AMUNDSEN. Home?
SCOTT. The thought of home keeps him moving. All of us.
The people we shall see there—the things we'll do—memories.
(*Kathleen enters* D. *to one side and takes a position there. She carries a*
small sculpture on its working tripod, covered with a wet cloth. She wears
a smock over a different dress from the one we saw in the first act. From its

53

pockets she takes out tools, and begins to work. She looks, if possible, younger — perhaps her hair is down.) I can't — I can't decide whether it's good to let them dwell on it. It gives them an incentive, yes, but sometimes — it also makes them tense and moody. I suppose though that nothing I could say or do — could possibly stop them from thinking of home . . .

KATHLEEN. (*Gaily.*) Captain Scott! (*Scott turns to see her.*)

AMUNDSEN. I tell you truly, English . . .

KATHLEEN. What a pleasant surprise to see you again!

AMUNDSEN. You would have been kinder to put a bullet through his head.

(*He touches Evans' forehead. Evans lurches unsteadily to his feet and stumbles off. Amundsen watches Scott and Kathleen for several moments. The wind and "Southern Lights" both fade.*)

SCOTT. (*To Kathleen, clearing his throat.*) Good — good afternoon, Miss Bruce. Mabel Beardsley was gracious enough to suggest — after the reception last evening — that I might come by and pay my respects. And so I've come — to pay them. (*Pause.*) I'm here.

KATHLEEN. (*A bit amused.*) Yes, you seem to be.

SCOTT. Yes.

KATHLEEN. Please forgive me. I'm rather distracted at the moment with this piece of clay.

SCOTT. Yes, yes, of course. Please — go right on with your work.

KATHLEEN. I'll only be a minute. There's a difficult bit here. (*Amundsen turns and goes. A silence while Kathleen works and Scott stares at her furtively, shifting his weight. She glances up, catching his eye. He is embarrassed; she laughs and goes back to her work.*) Are you aware that you've become the social lion of the season? Any affair that can flaunt you seems assured of success.

SCOTT. I find it all flattering, of course — but perhaps a bit out of proportion. (*Pause.*) What did you think of last night's?

KATHLEEN. I've a theory that all large social events fall under one of two broad categories; balloon ascensions and bear-baitings. According to their pretensions, of course.

SCOTT. Ah! (*Pause.*) And last evening?

KATHLEEN. Last evening was a bear-baiting posing as a balloon ascension. (*Scott chuckles uncertainly. After a moment, still working.*) Do you know anything about sculpture, Captain Scott? (*She moves away from her work, wiping her hands.*)

SCOTT. (*Cheerfully.*) Not a blessed thing. I'm afraid I've been in the Navy since I was thirteen.

KATHLEEN. I'm not sure that's a logical explanation.

SCOTT. It means, I'm afraid I've missed out on a few things I ought perhaps to know more about. Culture — and that sort of thing. Haven't had time for 'em.

KATHLEEN. Haven't you. Well, what do you think of this? (*Scott peers at her clay piece. It is a portrait bust, which appears to be in its early stages. We can see only the back of the head.*)

SCOTT. Of that? (*Pause.*) Well, I think — it's quite interesting. And rather different, too. And altogether good.

KATHLEEN. I think it's perfectly dreadful, myself. (*Pause.*) Everyone was really quite impressed with you last evening, weren't they?

SCOTT. I suppose so. They embarrassed me.

KATHLEEN. Did they? (*She begins working again at the sculpture.*)

SCOTT. I'm not sure I like being a somebody.

KATHLEEN. Oh, *I* should like to be somebody. I'd like to be incredibly famous. As long as I were proud of the way I'd got there. Are *you* proud?

SCOTT. I suppose I am. I got closer to the Pole than anyone before me. I only fell short a hundred miles or so.

KATHLEEN. Three hundred, I thought. *The Times* said . . .

SCOTT. Yes, well, it's so difficult to measure exact distances there.

KATHLEEN. Oh, I see.

SCOTT. (*Quickly.*) Yes.

KATHLEEN. Yes. (*Pause.*) Well then, no wonder you're quite full of yourself. I hardly blame you.

SCOTT. I never said I was full of myself at all, Miss Bruce.

KATHLEEN. No, but of course you are, just the same. And where's the harm in that? Only — forgive me, but — don't you ever feel just a bit of a sham?

SCOTT. What do you mean?

KATHLEEN. For capturing so much attention with what was, after all, a kind of stunt? A bear-baiting, if you like?

SCOTT. I don't think it was a stunt.

KATHLEEN. No? Then whose life did it enrich?

SCOTT. (*Calmly.*) My own.

KATHLEEN. I mean, what value did it have?

SCOTT. (*Amazed.*) Are you always so obsequious toward visiting celebrities?

KATHLEEN. Please don't change the subject.

SCOTT. You quite dislike me, don't you?

KATHLEEN. No, but I don't understand you. (*Pause.*) To me it's all nonsense. The South Pole! But I'd hoped from reading about you in the papers that at least you might turn out to be some sort of wild romantic, a visionary, a modern Columbus in furs and wind burns. But that's not at all the man I met last night.

SCOTT. And what was he?

KATHLEEN. Oh, medium height, strongly built. Not especially handsome, but terribly well-dressed, and with the most penetrating eyes. Dark blue — almost purple. A man whose outsides are all rocklike naval dignity, quite simple to sculpt. But whose insides are altogether different. Inside is — a fearful yearning. And — I think a kind of terror.

SCOTT. Of what?

KATHLEEN. Failure. (*Pause.*) Perhaps the yearning is for failure too. (*Pause.*) I was promised a smashing celebrity, and I got a haunted man.

SCOTT. It sounds as though you were terribly disappointed.

KATHLEEN. I can't decide.

SCOTT. Perhaps you're merely jealous, then.

KATHLEEN. Jealous? Of your kind of celebrity? Don't be idiotic.

SCOTT. Of my freedom. Because I don't fit so comfortably into little rooms as you do. Because a piece of clay that size isn't large enough to hold my dreams. Perhaps that's why you feel so compelled to challenge me, Miss Bruce.

KATHLEEN. And perhaps you're merely mad! Yes, I think you might have to be, to want to go to such a boring place.

SCOTT. A place where one might be killed at any instant could be called a great many things. Boring is not one of them.

KATHLEEN. Silly is. And melodramatic. And self-publicizing.

SCOTT. You needn't flatter me any further. I'll go.

(*Kathleen stops Scott with her voice before he can get far.*)
KATHLEEN. A place where you might be killed at any instant is not a place worth going to at all! That's merely vulgar. I should think it would make more sense to go to a place where one might suddenly, at any monent, become alive! (*Scott's back is to her, but he is listening.*) A daring expedition, deep into the darkest depths of a concert hall, or theatre! The dizzying ascent to the top floor of an art gallery—never before seen! Now *that* would be really dangerous! (*Scott turns back and looks at her.*) One might have to open one's eyes and *see,* and think, and *feel* and come out a different person altogether on the other side. But I suppose exploits like those don't often capture the headlines.

SCOTT. I've seldom met anyone who had such an elevated opinion of me.

KATHLEEN. Not of you.

SCOTT. Of my motives, then.

KATHLEEN. (*Moving towards her sculpture.*) Do you know what would frighten me, I think, if I were you? Just a little bit.

SCOTT. (*To Kathleen.*) What?

KATHLEEN. The way they make a sacred national hero of you in the schools now. They hold you up as an example to the children.

SCOTT. Oh, yes, I've heard about that. It's now their assigned pleasure to be bored by my exploits. But that's hardly frightening—unless you mean the danger of putting them to sleep.

KATHLEEN. No, I mean the danger of foolish ideas seeping into immature minds. The idea that daring is more to be respected than their own precious safety. That duty and honor should be held above an independent spirit, and that partiotism is more important than anything, more even than thinking for themselves. We shall have a whole generation of adventurers, Captain Scott, nurtured by you.

SCOTT. (*Taut with anger.*) Partriotism is not a joke, Miss Bruce. Honor and daring and sacred duty are not empty words. I despise to see them mocked by those who would scarcely be safe and warm in their homes, were it not for men who believed in them, and believed enough to offer their lives. Those words are our glory, they made the British Empire what it is today.

KATHLEEN. Then perhaps one day they will topple it, as

well. You may go to the Pole, Captain Scott, but what of your young worshippers left at home? What adventures will remain for them? How shall we ever satisfy so many? (*Bowers, Wilson and Oates enter, hauling the sled. Amundsen lounges across the sled, unseen by the men hauling it. They cross the stage and stop on the far side, exhausted, sinking in their tracks to catch their breath.*)

SCOTT. Let us make a pact, Miss Bruce—shall we? I shall leave off talking of sculpture, about which I've admitted I know nothing—and you will leave off this idle speculation about the nature of patriotism, of which you seem to know even less.

KATHLEEN. Oh dear! You don't frighten me, Captain Scott. Though you seem to be a most contrary man, and as different from me as chalk from cheese. In the event, I've made up my mind anyway, so our differences scarcely matter. I knew last night when I chose you.

SCOTT. (*After a pause.*) Chose me, Miss Bruce?

KATHLEEN. You are the man who will give me a son. (*Pause.*) With the benefit of wedlock, or without, as you wish.

WILSON. (*To Scott.*) Robert, shall I go back for Evans?

(*Scott stares at Kathleen in utter astonishment. The "Southern Lights" display flares up again sharply.*)

KATHLEEN. (*Calmly.*) You seem to have lost your powers of speech, Captain.

(*She turns to her sculpture.*)

WILSON. (*Turning to stare at Scott.*) Robert?

(*Amundsen and the others look at Scott.*)

SCOTT. Good lord. Good lord.

WILSON. (*Spinning Scott by the arm.*) Robert, what is *wrong* with you? You haven't heard a word I've said.

SCOTT. I—I . . .

WILSON. *Robert!*

SCOTT. What is it?

WILSON. It's Evans! You've got to make a decision. Should we haul Evans on the sled?

OATES. (*To Scott.*) He'll make any excuse to stop now. No-one has to retie his bootstraps three times inside an hour.

WILSON. Titus . . .

OATES. (*With pent-up frustration and anger.*) And you, Wilson! You're the worst—you know damn well what I'm saying is true, but you go on covering for him, making excuses—well it's just no good, Wilson, it just won't *go* any more! (*Scott looks back and forth from his men to Kathleen, in confusion. She is working at her sculpture, pulling chunks away.*) Half the time he doesn't make any sense at all! This morning he asked me which way was the lily pond. When I asked him what he was talking about he stared at me and laughed and said it was only a joke. (*Shouting.*) A joke! Well what do you call *that*?

WILSON. (*Equally angry.*) I call that a concussion of the brain. I call that the result of two severe falls, shock and exposure. He still has a dim memory of how he's supposed to act, and he's doing his best. His hands must be giving him agony, but I haven't *once* heard him complain, and neither have *you*, Mr. Oates—have you?

OATES. (*After a pause; somewhat embarrassed.*) No . . .

KATHLEEN. (*After a silence.*) My dearest Con. Something frightened me tonight. I was working late in my studio. I turned; Peter was there in the doorway, sleepy from bed. He said to me quite clearly, "Daddy won't be coming back." Oh love, I hear you say it's silly, but now I can't sleep. Where are you, and what is happening? (*Kathleen takes up her sculpture, which is now seen to be a bust of Scott, and exits, leaving the tripod behind. Scott follows her with his eyes. Amundsen, who has watched all in silence while seated on the sled, now rises and moves freely among Scott's men. They all remain somewhat stationary, relative to Amundsen, and only Scott notices him.*)

AMUNDSEN. (*Softly, near Bowers.*) Lord, this is a lonely place . . . (*Scott turns and sees Amundsen.*)

BOWERS. Lord, this is a lonely place. Look at those lights.

OATES. Day and night. Put me right off my food, they have.

WILSON. Beautiful. I'm fascinated by them.

OATES. They're hellish.

AMUNDSEN. (*After a silence; to Bowers.*) Listen! Listen . . .

BOWERS. That's the rummest thing of all to me. Do you hear that strange sound?

SCOTT. (*After a pause.*) I don't hear anything.

BOWERS. That's the one I mean. I can't get used to that, the sound of nothing. If we were here a hundred years I'd never get used to it.

SCOTT. I'd sooner silence than the wind . . .

AMUNDSEN. (*Near Oates.*) Do you suppose anyone knows we're here?

OATES. Do you think anyone knows we've failed, or even cares?

WILSON. (*Unconvincingly.*) Of course they know. Of course they care.

BOWERS. We could be on another planet.

OATES. It'd have to be Jupiter. That's a cold one too, I think. (*The "Southern Lights" soar even higher and brighter, flaming in different sheets of color.*)

WILSON. Look, the relief party must be at One-Ton Depot by now. If we're behind schedule they'll come out after us. They'll meet us.

BOWERS. Weather permitting, of course.

WILSON. Of course. (*Bowers takes the theodolite and attaches it to Kathleen's sculpture tripod. He takes a sighting.*)

AMUNDSEN. (*Firmly.*) I don't think so. (*The others turn in surprise, towards Scott. Amundsen stands beside him.*) I think they'll stop there, and wait.

BOWERS. Why, Captain?

SCOTT. There's four hundred miles of open land between us and them. If they come out too early, they take a chance of missing us in the intervening terrain.

AMUNDSEN. It's useless looking for the relief party to save us —

SCOTT. We shall have to do it on our own. (*He looks at Amundsen; he is frightened by his presence but helpless.*)

WILSON. Look, we're almost on schedule! We've talked about this a hundred times; there's no point thrashing it out again. We've just got to play it through.

BOWERS. But — what do you think it'll be like — getting back?

OATES. What do you mean?

BOWERS. I mean coming in second. Losing.

AMUNDSEN. It'll be all over the papers soon, about the Norskies.

BOWERS. What will they think?

AMUNDSEN. Will they even care?

OATES. Or will they think we were fools to come at all?

AMUNDSEN. They'll think we failed them.

OATES. I know them—they'll turn on us—

BOWERS. (*Moving back to the sled with the tripod and theodolite.*)—you just count on it, both houses of Parliament *and* the Press, they'll damn the expense and the waste.

OATES. We left heroes and we'll come back fools.

AMUNDSEN. We'll look ridiculous—

BOWERS. —and the *navy* will look ridiculous—

OATES —and we'll never hear the end of it! "Oh yes—you were with Scott, weren't you—?"

AMUNDSEN. (*To Scott, sharply.*) "The ones who were *second* . . . !"

SCOTT. No! (*Pause.*) What they'll think is that we've done the longest march on record and that we've got to the Pole and back again, as we said we would, and they can be damned proud of the first Englishmen to do it, or to hell with them all! (*He turns away, angrily, searching the distance for Evans.*)

AMUNDSEN. But something is wrong, isn't it, Scott? Something is terribly wrong and you know it . . .

SCOTT. Bowers, give me the telescope. (*Bowers hurries to open a crate, seizes the telecope and gives it to Scott.*)

AMUNDSEN. It's Evans, he's not coming, *why* . . . ?

WILSON. What is it?

AMUNDSEN. Something is wrong.

SCOTT. (*Sighting quickly.*) What the devil is he . . .

AMUNDSEN. Something is wrong.

SCOTT. I could swear he's not moving. I'm almost sure of it.

BOWERS. Is he down?

SCOTT. (*Puzzled.*) Kneeling, I think.

AMUNDSEN. Something is wrong . . .

SCOTT. (*After a pause.*) Now stumbling about—now . . . ! (*Frantically.*) Christ Jesus.

(*Scott drops the telescope on the ground, sets off running, and exits. Oates and Bowers follow as quickly as they can, Oates limping. Wilson starts to follow, runs back, takes a blanket from the sled, then hurries off after the others. Amundsen watches them go. He picks up the telescope, crosses back to the sled and drops it in a box. He claps his hands twice, sharply. Evans enters, whirling past Amundsen in a dizzy spinning dance that carries him* C., *where he collapses on his knees. Before Evans's motion is completed, Amundsen steps in front of the sled and picks up the traces. He hefts them to his shoulders, surges forward powerfully, and hauls the sled off. Evans has removed his coat, hat, and mittens. His remaining clothes are in disarray. His hands are purple and splotchy, the fingers so stiff they can barely be bent. Black streaks shoot up his wrists and forearms. Blood trickles from one ear. He sways gently on his knees and sings.*)

EVANS. (*Tonelessly.*) "Eternal father, strong to save,

Whose arm doth bind the restless wave . . .

Whose arm doth bind the restless wave..."

(*He unlaces his boots with great effort, and struggles to get them off.*)

"Who bids't the mighty ocean deep

Its own appointed limits keep,

O hear us when we cry to Thee

For those in peril on the sea.

O Christ, whose voice the waters heard

And hushed their raging at Thy word . . . "

(*Scott runs on and stops, staring at Evans.*)

SCOTT. (*Out of breath.*) For the love of God, Evans . . .

EVANS. (*Brightly.*) Oh hullo. Come in and close the door behind you. Tea is on.

SCOTT. (*Taking a step closer.*) Get up at once.

EVANS. Don't touch anything, I've just got it straight. (*He lines his boots up neatly.*)

SCOTT. I said get . . .

EVANS. (*Sharply.*) No! Stay you there! (*Scott stops, surprised.*) Everything's in order, you'll muck it up.

SCOTT. Evans—I want to help you. You've got to be covered.

EVANS. You keep your bloody distance, damn your eyes!

(*Wilson enters carrying the blanket, followed by Bowers; both out of breath. Oates, limping badly, enters last.*)

WILSON. Lord.

BOWERS. (*Staring towards Evans.*) Taffy—what's happened to you?

EVANS. (*Snatching a knife from a sheath at his belt.*) I will open the first man that crosses that floor. (*To Scott.*) I said close that door behind you! Close and bolt it, man.

OATES. Christ—he's stark raving mad . . .

BOWERS. Taff—you'll listen to me. (*He kneels in front of him.*) It's Birdie. Don't you know me, Taff?

(*Evans suddenly raises the knife to his own throat. Bowers moves back away from him.*)

SCOTT. Evans, put down the knife and we'll talk.

EVANS. (*Looking around.*) Two, three, four. This will never do. There are too many, too many altogether. Well then let's change, we're late for chapel as it is. (*He pulls his shirts over his head quickly, then holds the knife again to his throat. He is now barechested. He scrambles to his feet.*)

WILSON. Edgar, don't! (*To Scott, desperately.*) He's got to be covered! He can't stand there like that! (*Scott motions the others to surround Evans. They move cautiously, keeping a good distance so as not to alarm him.*)

EVANS. Sssh! They like their sleep of a Sunday morning, the old ones do. They'll hear us soon enough, look you, all this tramping about. They'll be waking, they'll be calling for their breakfast. (*He smiles.*) Smell! (*He sniffs.*) Can you smell that? That's scones, that is. If we've got everything tidy before services we can have ours with butter and honey. O sweet mother — I can smell them baking . . . (*Evans lowers the knife, swaying. Suddenly he gives a long, anguished scream, clutching his head. He tumbles over, moaning, as if having convulsions, and rolls across the ground with terrifying energy. The others rush forward and seize him. He struggles violently, snarling and spitting like an animal. At last he is restrained and seems to calm slightly, though he trembles very violently. Wilson throws the blanket over him. The following lines all come very quickly, and overlap.*)

WILSON. We've got to get him to the sledge, set up the stove — Lord, I've forgotten my kit . . .

EVANS. (*Moaning.*) Hot — it's so hot . . .

WILSON. His brain is haemorrhaging . . .

EVANS. Mother, help me I'm burning alive . . .

WILSON. What happened, Evans? Can you hear me? What happened? Did you fall again? Did you fall? Did you strike your head?

EVANS. (*Terrified.*) Who's there?

SCOTT. Oates, Bowers — run on back. Set up the tent as best you can, light the stove. Wilson and I will follow. Bill let's get him on his feet. (*Oates and Bowers turn to go. Bowers pauses, reluctant to leave Evans. They both hesitate, looking on, as Scott and Wilson lift Evans to his feet.*)

WILSON. Tell me what it feels like.

EVANS. Like sleep. Like dreams.

SCOTT. Listen to me, Evans—can you walk?

EVANS. Yes—so hot . . .

SCOTT. Are you sure?

EVANS. Hot . . . (*They support Evans as he staggers a few steps. His head is lolling from side to side. Suddenly he snaps it back, erect.*) Like fire! (*He screams.*) Like fire! (*He turns, clutching Scott's coat at the throat. He sees Scott, and for a terrible instant recognizes him.*) Scott—you've done me . . . (*His eyes, still staring, now roll up. A noise comes from the back of his throat, and a great gush of blood bursts from his mouth. He falls backward to the ground, thrashes for a moment, then is still.*)

WILSON. Eddie! (*He kneels, puts his ear to Evans's chest.*) Eddie, don't! For God's sake, don't! Please fight, please. Stay conscious! (*He pounds on Evans's chest, then listens again for a heartbeat. He tries this a second time, frenzied, irrational.*) Evans! (*He pulls Evan's body up to him and shakes him violently by the shoulders in his frustration. A long wail.*)

Evannnnnnns! (*A long silence. Wilson slumps over Evans, weeping softly, hugging the body. The others stand or kneel, staring.*)

OATES. Lord have mercy on us, Christ have mercy on us, saints have mercy on us all . . .

SCOTT. (*Moving to Wilson.*) It's over, Bill. It's over now.

OATES. (*In a whisper.*) Lord have mercy on us, Christ have mercy on us, saints have mercy on us all . . .

SCOTT. It wasn't your fault, it was mine. (*Wilson looks up, uncomprehending.*) You've got to get up now.

OATES. Lord have mercy on us, Christ have mercy on us, saints have mercy on us all . . .

(*Bowers kneels beside Evans and arranges the blanket about him.*)

SCOTT. (*To Wilson, gently.*) We've got to go now. We're going home. (*Scott helps Wilson to stand. Wilson hugs Scott, his shoulders shaking. Scott pats his back.*) Now we're all going home . . . (*Wilson breaks away and moves upstage. Scott kneels beside the body. Bowers shifts Evans's head and shoulders from his own lap into Scott's, then rises.*)

BOWERS. Good-bye, Taffy . . . (*Bowers moves upstage and stands near Oates, the two of them turning away from Scott and Evans. The wind and the "Southern Lights" fade away. The stage goes colder, darker. Scott cradles Evans in his arms. Before this tableau is completed Kathleen appears and moves towards Scott.*)

KATHLEEN. Con? (*Scott looks at her dully.*) Say good night to Peter.

SCOTT. Yes—good night, Peter. Sleep well, darling . . .

(*Kathleen picks up one or two items of Evans's clothing, amused at the mess he's made.*)

KATHLEEN. He's starting to teethe. Today for the first time it hurt to nurse him. He's so greedy for life.

SCOTT. Suddenly I feel terribly old . . .

KATHLEEN. You're not old. (*She kneels beside him, smoothes Evans's hair.*)

SCOTT. (*Still dazed.*) But can I be a real father to him, when he's growing up?

KATHLEEN. Honestly, Con. Sometimes this silly obsession with age! Two years ago you told me you were too old to ever marry—at thirty-nine!

SCOTT. (*Wiping the blood from Evans's face.*) The world is a very casual place. You wake up one day, and it's gone, you're just past it, and you might have dreamed the entire thing. (*Pause.*) I'm quite sure that must be the way it happens.

KATHLEEN. If it's your career—you needn't fear he'll hold you back. I can look after him myself.

SCOTT. I have no money, Kath, no position of any real meaning. Oh, a name perhaps. What sort of legacy is that? If I should fail him . . .

KATHLEEN. Con. You'll have many sons, and all of them will prosper.

SCOTT. Do you swear it?

KATHLEEN. Yes, I do.

SCOTT. Then I believe you. (*One by one Bowers, Oates and Wilson slip away and exit. Scott, Kathleen and Evans are left alone in a small circle of light, as the stage around them grows darker, blue shadows creeping in.*)

KATHLEEN. I think until Peter was born I was never fully in love with you. I loved you, yes, but I wasn't *in* love with you. I always looked upon you as a sort of—I don't know—a probationer. But he sprung something from me I'd never been willing to give. All those months when he was riding under my heart, the same food of blood. It was a sea change, Con—from the moment he was born I fell passionately in love with you.

SCOTT. I think I loved you because I knew you didn't need

65

me. You were complete in yourself, like one of your sculptures. You didn't give a damn I'd gone to the Antarctic and been in *The Times,* and that excited me no end.

KATHLEEN. I was just another challenge. One more piece of unexplored territory.

SCOTT. I was determined to make you need me — I thought, if she hasn't any use for a husband, she does for a son. (*Pause.*) I mean to be a good father, Kath. I may have a late start, but I shall work all the harder.

KATHLEEN. I know you will. It's time he was asleep. (*She passes Evans back to Scott.*)

SCOTT. Yes. Good night to you, Peter Markham Scott.

KATHLEEN. I'm fiercely proud to've made your son. I'm impatient for him to be grown, and know what sort of man he has for a father. (*Kathleen kisses Scott's forehead and rises: she picks up Evans's boots, then exits slowly.*)

SCOTT. (*Softly.*) Good night, love...

(*Amundsen enters and stands watching Scott. The wind is heard. Looking at Evans.*) No use to try and give him a proper burial. The ground's like granite.

AMUNDSEN. Scott.

SCOTT. We'll leave him where he lies. In time the snow and ice will cover him, and the wind be his true marker.

AMUNDSEN. (*Moving closer.*) Scott!

SCOTT. (*Dully.*) What?

AMUNDSEN. Get up.

SCOTT. Yes . . . (*Wilson, Bowers, and Oates enter upstage, carrying the tent, stove, and several boxes. Wearily they set up the tent. The sled remains off. Bowers is snowblind, and has a rag tied over his eyes. He fumbles badly and needs considerable help from Wilson. Oates is limping horribly. He makes no effort to help with the tent, but simply lies down inside it. A thick blue haze fills the stage, and the men must struggle against the wind as they work.*)

AMUNDSEN. For two weeks since Evans died, you've walked as if you slept. Now the men are dying on their feet. Get up and march, Scott.

SCOTT. (*Still sitting.*) Yes, must keep marching — only forty miles left now.

AMUNDSEN. The stench of gangrene is in the tent. Oates's feet are destroyed. Bowers is snowblind.

SCOTT. (*Lurching to his feet.*) Only forty, do you hear me? By God I've almost got them home! (*Bowers goes into the tent and lights the stove. A warm glow fills the tent area. He moves to cradle Oates in his lap. Outside, Wilson looks up, studying the sky.*)

AMUNDSEN. The sky is darkening. If the storms come now you'll be finished. Oates is slowing you down, just as Evans did. You must make a decision.

SCOTT. Oates hasn't marched fifteen hundred miles to die here. Not like this, not when we're so close. You took Evans, but you won't take Oates.

WILSON. (*Moving to Scott.*) Hopeless. I can't see a thing through these clouds. We're in for a bad blow.

SCOTT. (*Shouting at Amundsen.*) I said you won't take Titus! You hear me?

WILSON. (*Taking Scott's arm.*) Robert? What is it?

SCOTT. (*Lunging.*) I won't let you, you bastard! (*Wilson holds Scott back.*)

WILSON. (*Struggling with Scott.*) Robert, stop it! There's no one there.

SCOTT. (*Shouting.*) Look at him! He's standing there, he's taunting me!

WILSON. There's no-one! (*He turns Scott and shakes him.*) *Do you understand?*

SCOTT. (*After a pause.*) Yes.

WILSON. Calm yourself.

SCOTT. (*Hesitantly.*) Yes.

WILSON. Are you all right now?

SCOTT. I'm all right.

WILSON. The temperature has dropped to minus forty. A storm's blowing. We'll sit tight and set a course when it clears. Are those your orders?

SCOTT. Yes. It's the right thing to do. We'd lose our markers in the snow.

WILSON. Then let's go in.

SCOTT. Yes . . . (*Scott and Wilson start towards the tent. Behind them Amundsen picks up Evans's wrists and stands holding them, watching Scott.*)

WILSON. Robert . . . (*He stops.*) I just want you to know that—if we were sitting right now in my garden in Cheltenham—and you asked me again to come here . . .

SCOTT. I know it, Bill.

WILSON. (*Nodding.*) I'd better tend Oates's feet again.

(*Wilson goes into the tent. Scott looks back at Amundsen. Amundsen drags Evans slowly away, exits. Scott enters the tent.*)

BOWERS. Snow?

WILSON. (*Kneeling by Oates.*) Soon. How is he?

BOWERS. He slips in and out. (*Oates moans softly.*)

WILSON. Let's have a look then. (*He tries to pull off Oates's left boot. Oates groans.*) It's swollen. I'll have to cut the boot. (*Wilson takes a scalpel from his kit and cuts Oates's boot down the side. He tugs it off, revealing a bloody and bandaged foot. Oates moans sharply and goes limp.*)

BOWERS. He's fainted.

WILSON. Lord. (*Shocked.*) His toes have come off in the boot — three of them — flesh off the bone like a glove. (*To Scott.*) Medical kit!

(*Scott hands the kit to Wilson, who removes a vial and syringe and prepares an injection.*) I can give him an injection of morphine, that's about it. (*Scott helps him to roll up Oates's pants leg and underlegging, exposing blackened flesh. Wilson injects the thigh.*) There. I don't think there's much feeling from the knee down. The pain is gangrene creeping into the thigh muscles.

SCOTT. What are his chances?

WILSON. If I keep him pumped full of morphine? He may be able to hobble another week. Only because he's as strong as a bull. Another man would've collasped days ago. After that? I don't know — perhaps if he were on the sledge — if we had the strength to pull it . . .

SCOTT. But what are his chances?

WILSON. He hasn't any. Not a hope.

SCOTT. Even if we carry him?

WILSON. This kind of decay is irreversible. If we tried to carry him the effort, weak as we are, could kill us all. It's a horrible thing to say, but we were lucky with Evans. With Titus — he's already slowed us down so badly, well — if he doesn't die within the next few days we're going to be in a very desperate position, Robert.

SCOTT. Does he know it?

WILSON. In his heart, perhaps. But you know Titus — he'll

march until he drops.

BOWERS. (*After a pause; quietly.*) Wilson—how much opium in your kit?

WILSON. (*Looking in the kit.*) In tablets, a hundred and twenty of opium, and one vial of morphine. Enough to last him perhaps ten days.

BOWERS. I wasn't thinking of Titus at the moment. (*They look at Bowers.*) That's thirty tablets each, and the morphine. That's enough for a lethal dose, if you took it all at once, isn't it?

WILSON. I'm not even going to listen to this.

BOWERS. All I'm suggesting is that each of us has the right to end it if he sees fit, and if it comes to that. Quiet, peaceful, and with dignity. I just don't want to lose my mind! That would be the worst, to go without knowing why, or even who you are. To die like an animal. I say we divide up those drugs now.

WILSON. No.

BOWERS. Why not?

WILSON. Because it hasn't come to that yet, and I won't give you the means.

BOWERS. As a doctor?

WILSON. As your friend.

BOWERS. Damn it, Wilson, we're entitled! Did you see Evans's face?

WILSON. (*Angrily.*) If you have the means to end it at any moment, then there's little reason not to! You can simply take the easy way out. Well, that's not going to pull us through, none of us! It's only going to sap our will, and we might as well be dead now. I absolutely refuse.

SCOTT. I—I agree with Birdie. (*Wilson stares at him in disbelief.*) Each man has the right to do as he sees fit—I won't deny that to anyone. Divide the drugs.

WILSON. Do you think I like to see a man dying under my eyes when I can't lift a finger to save him? But I've got to think of the ones that *might* be saved, and not the one who's certainly lost. And you want me to help you murder yourselves!

SCOTT. I'm sick of playing God, Wilson! I won't have it anymore, not even from you.

WILSON. Is that an order?

SCOTT. I'm afraid you make me insist.

WILSON. Then I'm afraid too. (*Bitterly.*) And I want it clearly recorded in the journal that it was over my objections, and that I strongly warned against it.

SCOTT. Agreed. (*Wilson pushes the kit towards Scott, who opens it and removes two bottles of pills. He puts one in Bowers' fumbling hands, and offers the other to Wilson, who looks angrily away. This bottle Scott drops in his parka pocket. He looks up again at Wilson.*) Bill. Is there any doubt in your mind that Titus is dying? I mean any whatsoever?

WILSON. He may live a week. No longer.

SCOTT. Then I have no choice. (*Scott takes a syringe and a vial from the medical kit. With his hands trembling, he fills the syringe. Wilson and Scott stare at each other across Oates's sprawled body.*) Not this time . . .

WILSON. (*Quietly.*) There's always a choice, Robert.

SCOTT. Not for the rest of us.

BOWERS. What is it? What's happening?

WILSON. (*To Scott.*) Has it come to this, then? (*Pause.*) I recall a friend who couldn't bear the thought of hurting dogs.

BOWERS. (*Fearfully, uncertainly.*) Captain . . . ? (*Scott leans over Oates's leg with the syringe. He touches the leg with his free hand. He looks up at Wilson, who stares at him but does not move. Scott trembles; the needle wavers over the skin. Oates groans suddenly and shifts his weight in Bowers' lap. He is coming back to consciousness. Scott stares at Oates. He lowers the syringe, hiding it along one leg.*)

BOWERS. I think he's coming round.

OATES. (*Very weakly, almost inaudibly.*) Hello, Birdie. What day is it?

BOWERS. (*Straining to hear.*) What? (*Oates pulls Bowers's head down near his lips.*)

OATES. What day?

BOWERS. Why it's . . . (*To Scott.*) He wants to know, what's the day?

SCOTT. It's the sixteenth. Thursday — or Friday. (*He slips the syringe back into the medical kit. Oates laughs.*)

WILSON. What is it, Titus? What's funny?

OATES. (*Coughing.*) It's my birthday! Today is my bloody birthday!

BOWERS. (*Managing a laugh.*) You old bastard! You're thirty-two.

70

WILSON. Happy birthday, Soldier.

OATES. Thank you, Wilson. I was hoping — for a surprise party — bit of cake, tot of whisky, the odd cigar. (*He struggles to sit up.*)

BOWERS. I'll stick a candle in your biscuit.

OATES. Always a sport, Birdie.

BOWERS. How are you this morning?

OATES. Well, last night before I went to sleep, I made a wish. I prayed I wouldn't wake up. I've never once got what I really wanted for my birthday.(*He turns to Scott.*) If you'd leave me behind in my bag, that would do very nicely for a gift. And you'd all make better time.

WILSON. (*Pouring a mug of tea.*) Well, it's blowing a blizzard today, so none of us is going anywhere. Drink this. (*Oates drinks, then makes a face.*)

OATES. God, that's awful. Birdie — did you piss in the tea again?

BOWERS. Fine thing, when a man can't relieve himself out of doors.

OATES. (*After a pause.*) Listen to the wind. Spearing right through the tent.

BOWERS. (*After a pause, softly.*) In London, it's the verge of spring.

SCOTT. Yes . . .

SCOTT. Take a boat on the Serpentine, eh?

BOWERS. It gives me a kind of fever to think of it.

SCOTT. The whole world turned green and soft, and the rain warm again . . .

BOWERS. Soft mud.

WILSON. Ladies in their yellow dresses and bonnets, like crocuses.

SCOTT. The children . . .

OATES. (*After a pause.*) Bloody nuisance of a season, you ask me. Never could abide it. I never wanted to be any place but where I was. (*He looks at his foot. Pause. To Scott.*) How far are we from One-Ton Depot?

SCOTT. I make it only forty miles now.

OATES. (*To Wilson.*) Another sip of Birdie's tea. (*Wilson hands him another mugful. Oates drinks deeply and gratefully.*) Absolutely disgraceful. (*With a great effort, he is able to stand. He leans on*

71

Wilson's shoulder for support.) Do you know—I haven't had a decent cup of tea since I entered the service? (*Quickly.*) I'm just going outside. I may be some time. (*Oates stumbles out of the tent and hurries away, staggering and then righting himself against the wind. As Oates comes out of the tent, the sound of the wind suddenly leaps up very loud, like the noise of a jet taking off.*)

SCOTT. (*Crying out.*) Oates! (*He scrambles out of the tent, Oates is already out of sight. Scott has difficulty seeing or even standing outside the tent. He tries to shout above the roar of the wind.*) Oates, come back! Oates! Ooooatesss! (*He is pushed to his knees by the wind. He buries his face in his hands. Amundsen enters. Scott looks up, and peers at Amundsen through the blue haze. Tlhe wind diminishes.*) Titus . . . ?

AMUNDSEN. A brave man. His body will never be found.

SCOTT. What have I done? I slaughter them one by one.

AMUNDSEN. No time for pity, least of all for yourself. (*Scott takes the bottle of pills from his pocket.*)

SCOTT. It's over, isn't it. All but the last bit.

AMUNDSEN. While there are players left on the field? Come, Scott—don't you want to play?

SCOTT. I'm very tired . . .

AMUNDSEN. Play the game.

SCOTT. No.

AMUNDSEN. Play the *game!*

SCOTT. I don't give a damn any more! Leave me alone.

AMUNDSEN. You wish you didn't, but you never had any choice. You are who you are.

SCOTT. (*Bitterly.*) It was my own choice that brought us here. My own choice that rejected the dogs. That kept us from turning back when we could.

AMUNDSEN. But not that cut the hand. Not that killed Oates.

SCOTT. (*Fiercely.*) You won't deny me the choice that's still left me! (*He shakes the bottle of pills.*) My own *choice* even now.

AMUNDSEN. You have only forty miles to safety.

SCOTT. I can do the arithmetic as well as you. It's bitter but simple. Paraffin for four days, food for six. The last depot and the relief party are eight days away at this pace. We're just too weak, too slow.

AMUNDSEN. What is food, next to the spirit? A man dies when he stops wanting.

SCOTT. (*Still kneeling.*) We all know it. We've known it since

72

Evans, I think. Only no one will say it. We walk in silence because any sound we made would be a shout of despair. We turn our faces against the darkness, we grope for the pulse of our hearts, and feel an idiotic pride that they're still throbbing. In the night we huddle together for warmth, but touching, we're still alone. Still alone.

AMUNDSEN. (*Gently.*) At last, I think you begin to understand the game.

SCOTT. (*Quietly.*) Help me. (*Looking up.*) Help me?

AMUNDSEN. There's no help I can give you.

SCOTT. They weigh so heavily. All the other lives.

AMUNDSEN. You have strength enough.

SCOTT. And this . . . ? (*He holds out the bottle of pills in his hand.*)

AMUNDSEN. That's for men who have no choice. (*Amundsen extends a hand. Scott hesitates, then puts his hand into Amundsen's. Their hands wrap together around the pills, and then Amundsen tugs Scott to his feet.*) Not the Pole, but here.

SCOTT. What?

AMUNDSEN. The single moment you were born to live. One place, the pattern revealed. Not the Pole, but here.

SCOTT. Yes . . . (*Amundsen withdraws his hand, with the pill bottle.*)

AMUNDSEN. You feared life had passed you by, that you couldn't keep pace with younger men. And yet, you see — it's the younger men who are falling by the wayside, and you who are still strong. You thought it was a kind of death at the Pole — yet I tell you, you were never so alive as now, and the moment you were born for is here. (*Pause.*) Live it well.

(*Amundsen turns and is suddenly gone. Scott goes back into the tent, where Bowers and Wilson lie curled up, half-asleep. He drags a crate to the downstage side of the tent and sits. He takes his journal and a pencil from his pocket, opens it, and writes.*)

SCOTT. Wednesday, twenty-first March. The one hundred and forty-first day. We've dragged forward, Birdie and Wilson and I, God knows how we've done it. We're only *eleven miles* from safety now. It might as well be a hundred for all the strength we have left, and to make matters worse, a terrible blizzard has pinned us down here. I am proud to say no more has been mentioned of the drugs. (*He stops writing and looks about.*) Birdie? Bill? Are you awake?

BOWERS. Awake, sir . . .

73

SCOTT. Don't let yourselves fall asleep.

WILSON. (*Mumbling.*) I won't. I'm feeling quiet alert.

SCOTT. Good. (*He turns back to his writing.*) Dear Mrs. Bowers, Dear Mrs. Wilson. If this letter is ever found—I am afraid it will reach you after one of the the heaviest blows of your lives. I write when we are very near the end of our journey, and I am finishing it in company with two gallant gentlemen, to one of you a son, to the other a husband. As our troubles have thickened they have remained splendidly hopeful, believing in God's mercy to you. If any blame can be attached, let it rest on my shoulders. My whole heart goes out to you in pity. Yours, R. Scott. (*Pause.*) Message to the Public. The causes of the diaster are these . . . (*Scott continues to immerse himself in his writing. He works with enormous concentration, his lips moving silently. He pauses only to try to warm his hands. The stage around the tent grows quite dark. The wind is steady but not very loud. Kathleen appears to one side, lit by a follow spot. She wears a soft-colored summer dress.*)

KATHLEEN. (*Simply.*) I was sitting on the deck of a mail steamer, bound for New Zealand to meet the *Terra Nova* when she returned. The Captain came and said he wanted to speak to me in his cabin. The poor old chap's hands were trembling when he said, "I've got some news for you, but I don't see how I can tell you." I said, "The Expedition?" "Yes." "Well, let's have it." And then he showed me the message. (*Pause.*) All those long weary days with no more news—and the thought that even what news I had was eleven months old. Being on shipboard, and out of wireless range for so long, I must have been one of the last in the world to know. Well—he was often that way about his secrets. (*Pause.*) I slept, or didn't, on the top deck, and the nights were beautiful with the moon. The Third Officer sat by me day and night, not really understanding but wanting to, and sorrowful, like a big dog. I found out later they thought I might throw myself over, not knowing I didn't believe I could find the dead by doing so. (*As Kathleen speaks, she moves quite near Scott, who still sits on his crate at the edge of the tent. She reaches out and gently takes the scarf from about his neck. He looks up at her and smiles.*) They told me in New Zealand that the headlines around the world were greater than for the *Titanic*, that the King himself led a solemn vigil of mourning at St. Paul's, that every bell in

Europe rang. (*She walks away* D., *folding the scarf neatly, holding it in both hands.*) I don't know what possible interest they thought those things could have for me, but perhaps they meant well. (*Pause.*) And later, of course, the King gave me a piece of paper, and some bits of metal with ribbons attached. (*She stares quietly out front as Scott addresses her.*)

SCOTT. My darling Kath—I want you to know I shall not have suffered any pain. We simply stop being. Therefore you mustn't imagine any great tragedy. You know I cherish no sentimental rubbish about remarriage. When the right man comes along to help you in life you ought to be happy again. I wasn't a very good husband, but I hope I shall be a good memory. Make the boy interested in natural history if you can. It is better than games and they encourage it in some schools. I know you will keep him in the open air. (*Pause. He turns to look at Bowers and Wilson.*) Birdie? (*Silence.*) Bill—are you there? (*Silence.*) Bill . . . (*Silence. He turns to Kathleen again.*) Try and make him believe in a God. At least it's comforting. (*Suddenly, and eerily, the sound of the waltz music heard at the beginning of the Act is heard again, mixed with the wind. Lights shift to high slanting beams; late afternoon of a summer's day. Amundsen appears in a follow spot, opposite Kathleen. He wears a casual suit, in light pastel tones, and carries a walking-stick.*)

AMUNDSEN. The world is changing, Scott. England, Norway, Europe—the Great War changed everything, you wouldn't know it today. It's a smaller place, but not a more neighbourly one. A frightened place, a world of shopkeepers and thieves. Where is the heroic gesture in such a world? The man who can keep his bread on the table is a hero. Where on such an earth are men who walk like gods? Dead and gone, with Columbus and Magellan. The names are words only, the maps all filled. Twenty years after your death, and they talk of flying over the Pole in aeroplanes. Flying, in aeroplanes! (*The music swells noticeably. Oates appears, looking fresh and relaxed in a blazer and straw boater. Evans appears, similarly dressed, on the opposite side of the tent.*)

OATES. (*Cheerfully.*) Captain Scott! (*Scott turns and looks at him.*) I made it through. I wasn't killed in the storm, you only thought I was. (*He grins.*) Really, it's no joke. They found me and brought me home.

SCOTT. (*In a whisper.*) No, it can't be . . .

OATES. But it is! Look, they've got plenty of hot food here, and soft cots. There's chocolate, and wine. Evans is here, too, and his hands are as good as new. Show him your hands, Taffy! (*Evans raises his hands towards Scott.*)

EVANS. Good as new!

SCOTT. Leave me alone — please . . . (*Kathleen and Amundsen turn towards Scott.*)

KATHLEEN. Last night when I woke I knew. I crept out and ran down to the beach.

AMUNDSEN. Ladies and gentlemen — Captain Robert Falcon Scott!

KATHLEEN. I swam out in a calm sea, as far as my strength would take me.

OATES. Captain, listen. I can show you how to get here, it's not hard. There's a secret pass, you could be here in an hour!

KATHLEEN. I thought, my son will love the nights, and he will love the sea.

SCOTT. Tell him — tell our boy that I said . . .

AMUNDSEN. Playing the game means treating your dogs like gentlemen, and your gentlemen like dogs.

OATES. Aren't you coming, Captain?

WILSON. (*Sitting up in the tent.*) I don't blame you, Robert. Only — could you see these letters get to my wife?

BOWERS. (*Also sitting up.*) I just don't want to lose my mind. That would be the worst.

EVANS. Oh thank God, sir! Thank you! You don't know what this means to me.

AMUNDSEN. English, you don't even know who you are.

WILSON. Lord — his toes have come off in the boot!

BOWERS. To go without knowing who you are. To die like an animal.

AMUNDSEN. You're the most dangerous kind of decent man.

KATHLEEN. Don't you ever feel just a bit of a sham?

WILSON. I want it recorded, it was against my objections! (*They all begin to approach Scott, slowly. The wind and the waltz music build crazily. The "Southern Lights" begin to swirl.*)

BOWERS. Like an animal.

OATES. He'll never keep up. He's too weak.

WILSON. You can simply take the easy way out.

BOWERS. Like an animal.

EVANS. Scott, you've done me.

KATHLEEN. I'm fiercely proud to have made your son.

AMUNDSEN. Live it well.

BOWERS. Each of us has a right to end it.

WILSON. Easy way out.

KATHLEEN. Fiercely proud.

AMUNDSEN. Live it well.

WILSON. Easy way.

EVANS. You've done me.

BOWERS. End it.

OATES. He's too weak.

WILSON. Easy way!

EVANS. Done me!

BOWERS. End it!

KATHLEEN. Proud!

AMUNDSEN. Live it well!

WILSON. Easy way!

EVANS. Done me!

OATES. Too weak!

BOWERS. End it!

SCOTT. (*Shouting loudly.*) No! (*They halt. The music and wind cease very abruptly. Scott speaks firmly, without fear.*) We can no longer help or hurt each other. I make my peace with you.

(*Oates, Evans, Bowers, Wilson and Kathleen begin to file away and exit, very slowly. The "Southern Lights" fade, as well as the general lights.*)

AMUNDSEN. Far away, on the Great Ice Shelf, your bodies lie still where they fell—perfectly preserved, fresh as life, magical. You, who were so afraid of aging! And every year as the Shelf builds itself outwards, you move a few feet closer to the edge, where the great chunks of iceberg break off into the sea.

SCOTT. (*Exhausted.*) Thursday, twenty-nine March . . .

AMUNDSEN. One day a great crystal barge will break away and carry you off, Scott, like a Viking king surrounded by his lieutenants. Then together you'll sail northwards at last, into warm seas, into the sun again. North, towards home . . .

SCOTT. For my own sake I do not regret this journey. We took risks, we knew we took them; things have come out against us, and therefore we have no cause for complaint. (*Amundsen's light fades. The lights close in to a spot on Scott's face.*) Had we lived, I should have had a tale to tell of the hardihood, endurance and courage of my companions which would have stirred the heart of every Englishman. These rough notes and our dead bodies must tell the tale. It seems a pity, but I do not think I can write more. (*Pause.*) Last entry. For God's sake look after our people.

The spot fades to a Black-out. The play is over.

"If Scott had reached the South Pole before Amundsen did and returned to England fit and smiling, he would have soon been forgotten by most of the English. It was not simply that five unusual men had died, though that meant something in 1913, before the casualty lists darkened the papers every morning and whole nations existed with death at their elbow. What catches and holds the imagination of the English is not successful achievement in the ordinary sense. What they cherish, even though most of them would immediately deny it, is any action, though it may be accounted a failure, that appears when it is recorded to be epic, that takes on a poetic quality, that haunts the mind like a myth. The long silence, the sudden tragic news, the idea of Scott and his companions 'nomed in that remote howling wilderness of snow and ice, all of it fired the imagination, and not only then, in 1913, but ever since."

J.B. Priestley
The Edwardians

(Reproduced by kind permission of the Rainbird Publishing Group Limited)

FURNITURE AND PROPERTY
LIST

See Production Notes for detailed
descriptions

ACT I

On stage:
Ship's spar with vast white fabric
attached

Off stage:
Sled with leather traces and tar-
paulin (Scott's Men)
In it: Wooden crates
Boxes of provisions
Axe
Tent
Portable stove
Cooking utensils
5 metal bowls, mugs, dishes,
cutlery
Food to include stew, tea, sugar,
tinned milk, biscuits
Matches
Water containers
Tripod
Theodolite with lens polisher
Teapot
Sextant
Thermometer (on side of sled)
Paraffin
Wooden medical kit, including
bandages, dressings, disinfec-

tant, scissors, various medi-
cines, bottles of pills, gauze,
scalpel, morphiné vials, syringes
Telescope
Spare clothing
Leather-bound sketch book
Sleeping-bags
Blankets
Odometer
Camera with long string and flash
Parcel containing scarf (Kath-
leen)
Bamboo pole with Norwegian
flag and leather pouch contain-
ing letter (Amundsen)

Personal:
Scott: notebook, pencil, pipe,
tobacco, matches, small British
flag
Bowers: chart book, pencil
Oates: rations list, pipe, tobacco,
matches
Wilson: small flat stone, sketch-
ing pencil, cigar, matches
Amundsen: flask

ACT II

Strike:
Tent, stove, several boxes

Set:
On sled: (representing dining-table): long tablecloth, five formal place settings, wine glasses, floral arrangement, menus, napkins
Inside sled: Scott's Antarctic clothing, blanket, telescope in crate, 5 dining-chairs

Off stage:
Sculpture of Scott's head covered with wet cloth, on tripod, sculpting tools (Kathleen)
Tent, stove, several boxes from sled (Wilson, Bowers, Oates)

Personal:
Evans: knife in sheath
Bowers: rag to cover eyes
Oates: bloodystained bandage on foot
Amundsen: walking-stick
Wilson: medical kit, with scalpel, vials, syringes, 2 bottles of pills
Scott: journal, pencil

LIGHTING PLOT

Property fittings required: slide Projector, chandelier
An open stage
PROLOGUE
To open: Darkness
Cue 1   After short pause   (Page 10)
              Bring slide projector into action until series complete,
                then brighten until last slide merges into sheet of
                white: cross-fade to spot on SCOTT

ACT I
To open: As close of Prologue
Cue 2   AMUNDSEN enters   (Page 13)
              Bring up spot on AMUNDSEN

Cue 3   AMUNDSEN: "Captain Robert Falcon Scott."   (Page 13)
              Bring up extra spot on SCOTT

Cue 4   SCOTT: "Afterwards I may rest?"   (Page 14)
              Bring up spot on KATHLEEN

Cue 5   KATHLEEN exits   (Page 15)
              Fade spots: bring up full stage lighting

Cue 6   OATES exits   (Page 18)
              Fade to spot on SCOTT

Cue 7   AMUNDSEN claps hands   (Page 18)
              Cross-fade to eerie colored glow

Cue 8   SCOTT: ". . . I don't know what I wanted."   (Page 21)
              Dim lighting, especially upstage; moonlight, leafy
                shadows

Cue 9   KATHLEEN exits   (Page 26)
              Cross-fade to overall cold evening light

Cue 10   The men eat in their tent   (Page 35)
              Slow fade of lighting on tent area

Cue 11   EVANS: "Tracks. Of dogs."   (Page 42)
              Lights shift abruptly, as if sun wheeling across at
                impossible speed

Cue 12	As men settle into positions for photo	(Page 45)
	Quick fade to silhouette effect: spot on KATHLEEN *as she enters*	
Cue 13	KATHLEEN: "By the spring."	(Page 45)
	Fade spot on KATHLEEN *to half: bring up spot on* SCOTT	
Cue 14	BOWERS takes photo	(Page 46)
	Increase lighting to blinding brightness: snap to black as AMUNDSEN *smiles at audience: bring up slide projector and hold until House Lights come up*	

ACT II

To open: Darkness

Cue 15	After short pause	(Page 47)
	Bring up slide projector, as Act I	
Cue 16	At end of slide sequence	(Page 47)
	Hold last slide: Lights come up to mysterious sparkling effect, resolving into chandelier: Lights up on scrim, dissolving slide, and to silhouette effect on dining-table	
Cue 17	As SCOTT and his Men sit	(Page 48)
	Bring up full lighting on dining-table	
Cue 18	WILSON: ". . . sauce with mushrooms . . ."	(Page 51)
	Eerie colored lighting on scrim and cyclorama ("Southern Lights"): take out chandelier	
Cue 19	EVANS exits	(Page 54)
	Fade "Southern Lights" into general lighting, concentrating on SCOTT *and* KATHLEEN	
Cue 20	WILSON: " . . . shall I go back for Evans?"	(Page 58)
	Bring up "Southern Lights"	
Cue 21	KATHLEEN exits	(Page 59)
	Fade concentration on SCOTT *and* KATHLEEN	
Cue 22	OATES: " . . . a cold one too, I think."	(Page 60)
	Increase "Southern Lights"	
Cue 23	BOWERS: "Good-bye, Taffy . . ."	(Page 64)
	Fade "Southern Lights": darken stage generally to cold light	
Cue 24	BOWERS, WILSON and OATES exit	(Page 65)
	Concentrate lighting on SCOTT, KATHLEEN *and* EVANS: *Blue shadows around them*	
Cue 25	WILSON, BOWERS and OATES enter	(Page 66)
	Bring up thick blue haze over whole stage	

Cue 26 BOWERS lights stove (Page 67)
Warm glow round tent area

Cue 27 SCOTT: " . . . causes of the disaster are (Page 74)
these . . ."
*Darken stage except around tent: bring up follow
spot on* KATHLEEN

Cue 28 SCOTT: "At least it's comforting." (Page 75)
*Cross-fade to high, slanting beams of light — late after-
noon of a summer's day: bring up follow spot on*
AMUNDSEN

Cue 29 The Men advance on SCOTT (Page 76)
Bring up "Southern Lights"

Cue 20 On general exit (Page 77)
*Slow fade of all lighting, including "Southern Lights"
and spots*

Cue 31 AMUNDSEN exits: "North, towards home . . ." (Page 77)
Fade to spot on SCOTT

Cue 32 SCOTT: "Look after our people." (Page 78)
Fade to Black-out

EFFECTS PLOT

PROLOGUE

Cue 1   At opening, after short pause   (Page 10)
Shudder of wind—repeat two times

Cue 2   For Slide 3   (Page 10)
Wind rising and subsiding

Cue 3   For Slide 5   (Page 10)
Increase wind

Cue 4   For Slide 9   (Page 10)
Increase wind to wild shrieking

Cue 5   SCOTT looks up   (Page 11)
Increase wind to climax, then cut abruptly

ACT I

Cue 6   AMUNDSEN: " . . . I give you—Robert Scott."   (Page 14)
Soft wind—continue until entrance of Men

Cue 7   OATES exits.   (Page 18)
Soft wind

Cue 8   SCOTT: ". . . I don't know what I   (Page 21)
         wanted."
Cross-fade wind to sound of trickling water

Cue 9   SCOTT: " . . . think kindly of me."   (Page 25)
Cross-fade crickets to soft wind

Cue 10   Lights fade on tent   (Page 35)
Increase wind slightly

Cue 11   SCOTT: " . . . let him do his best."   (Page 39)
Fade wind

Cue 12   EVANS: "Tracks. Of dogs."   (Page 42)
Sound of wind

Cue 13   As Men settle into position for photo   (Page 45)
Increase wind slightly

Cue 14   SCOTT: " . . . without the reward of priority!"   (Page 46)
Increase wind

Cue 15   After BOWERS takes photo   (Page 46)
Martial music, rising in volume: fade during
     intermission

ACT II

Cue 16   As Act opens   (Page 47)
            Waltz music, soft

Cue 17   Men give three cheers   (Page 51)
            Swell waltz music

Cue 18   AMUNDSEN enters   (Page 51)
            *Stop music abruptly: pause, then bring up sound
            of wind*

Cue 19   WILSON " . . . sauce with mushrooms . . . "   (Page 51)
            Fly out chandelier, slowly

Cue 20   EVANS exits   (Page 54)
            Fade wind

Cue 21   WILSON: "Shall I go back for Evans?"   (Page 58)
            Bring up sound of wind

Cue 22   BOWERS: "Good-bye, Taffy . . . "   (Page 64)
            Fade wind

Cue 23   AMUNDSEN enters   (Page 66)
            Bring up sound of wind

Cue 24   OATES comes out of tent   (Page 72)
            Increase wind suddenly, like a jet taking off

Cue 25   AMUNDSEN enters   (Page 72)
            Diminish volume of wind — steady but not very loud

Cue 26   SCOTT: "At least it's comforting."   (Page 75)
            Waltz music as at opening of Act II: continue wind

Cue 27   AMUNDSEN: "Flying in aeroplanes!"   (Page 75)
            Increase waltz music noticeably

Cue 28   Men advance on SCOTT   (Page 76)
            Build wind and waltz music "crazily"

Cue 29   SCOTT (*shouting*): "No!"   (Page 77)
            Snap off wind and waltz music

SLIDE PLOT

PROLOGUE

1. Moonlit seascape
2. Three-masted steamship at sea
3. Same ship in heavy seas
4. Ship trapped in pack ice
5. Ship far away
6. Endless plain of ice
7. Long grey mountain range, snow-capped peaks
8. Drifts of snow
9. Vast indefinite panorama of threatening sky and landscape

ACT I

10. Photo of *actual* Scott party

ACT II

11. The young Prince Edward (VII)
12. Street in Edwardian London
13. Croquet party
14. Henley Regatta
15. Edwardian children at play
16. A nanny and two little girls
17. Elegant restaurant
18. King Edward VII as an old man
19. Crowd on dock watching steamship

NEW PLAYS

★ **SHEL'S SHORTS by Shel Silverstein.** Lauded poet, songwriter and author of children's books, the incomparable Shel Silverstein's short plays are deeply infused with the same wicked sense of humor that made him famous. "…[a] childlike honesty and twisted sense of humor." —*Boston Herald.* "…terse dialogue and an absurdity laced with a tang of dread give [*Shel's Shorts*] more than a trace of Samuel Beckett's comic existentialism." —*Boston Phoenix.* [flexible casting] ISBN: 0-8222-1897-6

★ **AN ADULT EVENING OF SHEL SILVERSTEIN by Shel Silverstein.** Welcome to the darkly comic world of Shel Silverstein, a world where nothing is as it seems and where the most innocent conversation can turn menacing in an instant. These ten imaginative plays vary widely in content, but the style is unmistakable. "…[*An Adult Evening*] shows off Silverstein's virtuosic gift for wordplay…[and] sends the audience out…with a clear appreciation of human nature as perverse and laughable." —*NY Times.* [flexible casting] ISBN: 0-8222-1873-9

★ **WHERE'S MY MONEY? by John Patrick Shanley.** A caustic and sardonic vivisection of the institution of marriage, laced with the author's inimitable razor-sharp wit. "…Shanley's gift for acid-laced one-liners and emotionally tumescent exchanges is certainly potent…" —*Variety.* "…lively, smart, occasionally scary and rich in reverse wisdom." —*NY Times.* [3M, 3W] ISBN: 0-8222-1865-8

★ **A FEW STOUT INDIVIDUALS by John Guare.** A wonderfully screwy comedy-drama that figures Ulysses S. Grant in the throes of writing his memoirs, surrounded by a cast of fantastical characters, including the Emperor and Empress of Japan, the opera star Adelina Patti and Mark Twain. "Guare's smarts, passion and creativity skyrocket to awesome heights…" —*Star Ledger.* "…precisely the kind of good new play that you might call an everyday miracle…every minute of it is fresh and newly alive…" —*Village Voice.* [10M, 3W] ISBN: 0-8222-1907-7

★ **BREATH, BOOM by Kia Corthron.** A look at fourteen years in the life of Prix, a Bronx native, from her ruthless girl-gang leadership at sixteen through her coming to maturity at thirty. "…vivid world, believable and eye-opening, a place worthy of a dramatic visit, where no one would want to live but many have to." —*NY Times.* "…rich with humor, terse vernacular strength and gritty detail…" —*Variety.* [1M, 9W] ISBN: 0-8222-1849-6

★ **THE LATE HENRY MOSS by Sam Shepard.** Two antagonistic brothers, Ray and Earl, are brought together after their father, Henry Moss, is found dead in his seedy New Mexico home in this classic Shepard tale. "…His singular gift has been for building mysteries out of the ordinary ingredients of American family life…" —*NY Times.* "…rich moments …Shepard finds gold." —*LA Times.* [7M, 1W] ISBN: 0-8222-1858-5

★ **THE CARPETBAGGER'S CHILDREN by Horton Foote.** One family's history spanning from the Civil War to WWII is recounted by three sisters in evocative, intertwining monologues. "…bittersweet music—[a] rhapsody of ambivalence…in its modest, garrulous way…theatrically daring." —*The New Yorker.* [3W] ISBN: 0-8222-1843-7

★ **THE NINA VARIATIONS by Steven Dietz.** In this funny, fierce and heartbreaking homage to *The Seagull*, Dietz puts Chekhov's star-crossed lovers in a room and doesn't let them out. "A perfect little jewel of a play…" —*Shepherdstown Chronicle.* "…a delightful revelation of a writer at play; and also an odd, haunting, moving theater piece of lingering beauty." —*Eastside Journal (Seattle).* [1M, 1W (flexible casting)] ISBN: 0-8222-1891-7

DRAMATISTS PLAY SERVICE, INC.
440 Park Avenue South, New York, NY 10016 212-683-8960 Fax 212-213-1539
postmaster@dramatists.com   www.dramatists.com